Pockets of Freedom

UNLOCKING THE POWER OF INTUITIVE TEACHING AND LEARNING

D1522311

Sue Haynes, Phyl Brazee, and Lisa Plourde
Illustrations by Emily Bracale

Published by Wheatmark®
2030 East Speedway Boulevard, Suite 106
Tucson, Arizona 85719 USA
www.wheatmark.com

ISBN: 978-1-62787-836-4 (paperback)
ISBN: 978-1-62787-837-1 (ebook)
LCCN: 2020915654

Authors contact information:
Phyl Brazee: Phyllis.brazee@gmail.com
Sue Haynes: suewhaynes@gmail.com, CreativeMavericks.net

Bulk ordering discounts are available through Wheatmark, Inc. For more information, email orders@wheatmark.com or call 1-888-934-0888.

For Lisa Plourde—friend, colleague, mentor

1956–2013

Acknowledgments

The authors wish to thank:

Bonnie Lyons for cheering our project on, for her generous financial support for the book publication, and for her tribute to Lisa;

Rick Barter for his interview about Lisa;

Carol Chang for her tribute to Lisa;

Emily Bracale for her tribute to Lisa and for her delightful illustrations; and

Stuart Grauer for giving us his blessing to use his metaphor "Pockets of Freedom" for the title of our book!

And we gratefully acknowledge our students, who taught us so much!

Contents

Part I
Phyl: Teaching Is a Sacred Calling
7

Introduction
9

Theme 1

Theme 2

Theme 3

Contents

Theme 4

Weaving the Themes Together

**Part II
Lisa: "You Can Do It!"
33**

Introduction
35

Theme 1

Theme 2

Theme 3

Theme 4

Contents

Weaving the Themes Together

"The Class from Hell," 60

Conclusion
"You Can Do It!" 77

**Part III
Sue: Teaching with Joy**
81

Introduction
83

Theme 1

Seeing the Unique Potential in Each and Every Student Through Honoring Their Needs, Interests, and Passions, 89

Theme 2

Observing and Trusting Our Intuition Through Involving Our Hearts as well as Our Heads in Moment-to-Moment Decision-Making, 94

Theme 3

Evaluating Our Students Through Honoring Their Learning Process and How They Make Meaning in Their Lives, 100

Theme 4

Sharing Power in Authentic Ways Through Promoting Risk-Taking, Choice-Making, and Collaboration, 105

Weaving the Themes Together

Case Study of Christina, 112

Contents

Part IV
Neuroscience Support for Teaching
from the Heart, as well as the Head,
121

Introduction
123

The Invitation

My daughter Audrey and I played hooky once per year when she was in her earlier years. Not fishing. But Disneyland. Year after year this was our one-day respite from educational incarceration, our anecdote to sitting disease, our liberation from the rows and columns we refused to let define us. Never mind that I was a school official and supposed role model; I tried mightily to corrupt my daughter of the notion that schooling was not an act of free will. To hell with conventional wisdom about formal education; at least once per year we knew a world of playfulness with no experts, paragraphs with no topic sentences, and games with no officials. One in which we discovered our own patterns. Then back to school the next day with a gleam in our eyes.

Now many years later, I still wonder how, as teachers, we might find ways to add just a few such open spaces—little, renegade *pockets of freedom*—right in our own classrooms.

Stuart Grauer
"In Praise of Hooky" in *Fearless Teaching*

Preface

"Many programs are trying to effect educational reform from the outside in, but the greatest immediate power we have is to work to reform from the inside out. Ultimately, human wholeness does not come from changes in our institutions, it comes from the reformation of our hearts."

—Parker Palmer

Pockets of Freedom: Unlocking the Power of Intuitive Teaching and Learning celebrates the role of heart-based intuitive guidance in promoting authentic teaching and learning. We three authors share our stories about how our intuitive guidance informed our creation of "pockets of freedom" within our classrooms to support self-empowered learning in our students, a process involving profound honoring.

We, the authors, taught in public institutions that, for the most part, did not understand or support our relational teaching. However, we knew in our hearts that blindly following the current mechanistic philosophy of education would deny our souls and the souls of our students. We could not, would not, let that happen. So we dug deeply into what we truly believed about authentic teaching and learning and quietly, defiantly, created freedom spaces in our classrooms in support of this.

"Everyone talks about freedom. All around the world, different people, different races, different countries are fighting for freedom. But what is freedom? In America we speak of living in a free country. But are we really free? True freedom has to do with the human spirit. It is the freedom to be who we truly are."

—Don Miguel Ruiz

We, the authors, recognize that we all have an intrinsic authentic Self beyond the culturally cobbled together self that is influenced by the family, schooling, and the society into which we were born. This core is the illuminated self of the soul's inner awareness, tapped by the heart's intuitive wisdom. It is the development of this magnificent core that we have felt compelled to ignite and support in ourselves and in our students.

Our stories share how we strove to give our students the opportunity to become free from the conditioning which overshadowed their authentic selves—freedom to be who they truly were. By providing pockets of freedom within our classrooms, we offered spaces in which our learners were given the opportunity to discover and honor their hearts' intuitive guidance, their souls' leadings. By fostering each individual's unique profile of growth, we gave our learners the opportunity to develop strong agency by becoming self-guiding participants in their own learning and growth. Our stories share how we also gave our students many opportunities to revel in their unique expression and to delight in extending that beautiful self-awareness into the world.

We are older now. One of us has passed on; one has retired from formal teaching; and one continues a lifetime of tutoring individual students. Yet what we have in common is a desire to be authentic teachers. In these constrained times in the education of our children, it is so very important for wise souls to speak out, to share their hard-earned truths and wisdom about courageous empowering acts of teaching which defy traditional education's coercion toward artificial standardization.

Introduction

Pockets of Freedom: Unlocking the Power of Intuitive Teaching and Learning consists of teaching stories from three educators: Phyl Brazee, Lisa Plourde, and Sue Haynes. It is organized around a common set of beliefs shared by all three teachers. The following themes represent those beliefs:

- Seeing the unique potential in each and every student through honoring their needs, interests, and passions;
- Observing and trusting our intuition through involving our hearts as well as our heads in moment-to-moment decision-making;
- Evaluating our students through honoring their learning process and how they make meaning in their lives; and
- Sharing power in authentic ways through promoting risk-taking, choice-making, and collaboration.

The seed of the idea for the book grew from Sue's admiration of her remarkable teacher colleagues: Phyl, her professor and mentor for her master's degree in literacy at a public university, and Lisa, the seventh grade teacher of two of Sue's children in a public middle school. When Sue invited Phyl to coauthor the book with her, Phyl said yes, on the condition that Sue include her own teaching stories.

We three believed in and supported the empowerment of our students, maintaining this belief often within an educational climate antithetical to our beliefs:

- A climate increasingly restricted by the state and federal governments' obsession with standardized testing—*one size fits all.*
- A climate in which administrators felt increasing pressure to insist that teachers "teach to the test" in order to achieve test scores that benefitted schools' reputations and funding.
- A climate that denigrated intuition, insisting on prescribed analytical "one right answer" thinking.
- A climate that could see no place for authentic, heartfelt relational teaching.

Within this climate there was—and continues to this day to be—so little encouragement for the support of personhood growth. Students were—and continue to be—evaluated by how they have measured up to mandated curriculum and test standards, not by how authentic their personal learning integration has been.

We three refused to deny the honoring of each of our students. Toward this goal, we created pockets of freedom within our classrooms year after year. We persisted because our hearts would not be compromised.

Phyl

I taught for forty years in several higher education institutions that literally did not care at all about the environment in which teaching and learning occurs. There is so often no thought given to the physical space of teaching and learning at the college level: size of a classroom, whether there are roundtables for small group work rather than the rows and rows of right-handed desks, absolutely sterile walls, no plants, etc. I taught in classrooms that completely defied my teaching philosophy and beliefs, yet I persevered. Students did small-group work out in the hallway or in unused classrooms on the same floor; we created small groups by moving heavy furniture each class period, making sure to put it back at the end of each session.

Also, so much of college teaching is done via lectures—"pouring knowledge into students' empty vessels." I believed in a very different philosophy—engaging students in cocreating the curriculum and including their own life experiences within the hands-on experiences I created for each class session. In the end, it was all on me to create heart energy, both in terms of physical space and in terms of the teaching/learning process. In retrospect, I was able to give out heart energy and create sacred spaces over my entire career because I knew that my teaching philosophy and beliefs created pockets of freedom for my students and myself.

In the end, that's all I needed.

Lisa

Lisa was a seventh and fifth grade teacher in a small-town elementary school. She taught for twenty-seven years before her retirement in 2011 and sadly passed away in 2013. During Lisa's tenure as a fifth grade teacher, Sue had the privilege of interviewing her and observing in her classroom as well. Sue is the narrator of Lisa's section of this book.

In the face of increasing strictures about what and how she should teach, Lisa persisted in honoring every single student who walked into her classroom, promoting personal agency growth over "measuring up" and fitting in. When Sue asked Lisa what supported her in her mission despite her "feeling under a microscope—you know like the magnifying glass that the kids will put on the ant and the sun comes through and it starts to crisp the ant. Well, I was the ant, and I was increasingly feeling a little crisp around the edges," Lisa said. "I always got acknowledgement from the kids. Even if they couldn't verbalize it, they let me know things were working out fine." Informed by her heart's intuition, Lisa unstintingly created rich varieties of pockets of freedom in her classroom year after year.

Sue

My teaching journey has been eclectic. Master's degrees in both special education and literacy qualified me to teach in regular elementary classrooms, special education classrooms, and the Teacher Education Program of a college. And I was well qualified to hang out my own shingle at home.

Through sharing my stories, I hope to demonstrate how my focus on personhood empowerment with students in regular and special education classrooms, as well as in home tutoring, offered them freedom to learn in a manner most suited to their individuation. The alternative college in which I taught in the Teaching Education Program allowed me this freedom as has my home tutoring. As well, I was fortunate to have a supportive principal for my two-year tenure as a kindergarten teacher. My special education classes, however, challenged me to translate a holistic teaching approach within a behaviorist system of measurable goals and objectives. I "got away with" my unorthodox teaching because my students thrived in ways beyond expectations. In all the different classrooms I taught in, I rejoiced in creating pockets of freedom to promote growth of personhood in both myself and my students.

Our three sections of stories demonstrate that teachers *can* create pockets of freedom for their students, even within inhospitable environments. Our pockets of freedom sprang from a common set of beliefs that come from the heart, that demonstrate promotion of self-empowered agency, and that validate the power of intuition in generating authentic teaching and learning.

Part I

Phyl

"Teaching Is a Sacred Calling"

Introduction

Authentic teaching is a labor of love; it is a sacred calling; it is a lifelong commitment—at least it is to me! It calls us to live and work from our hearts as much as from our heads. It also calls us to have the courage of our convictions, especially in the face of bureaucracies that try to repress us. We need that courage to create pockets of freedom for ourselves and for our students.

I have taught for forty-three years, three as a public school remedial-reading teacher in grades kindergarten through ninth and forty years as a university professor in a variety of academic areas. I have loved every minute of these teaching experiences. As I moved into retirement, I came to realize through deep reflection what I most value in the act of teaching, what I will miss, and what I want to re-create in some way in my new life. In the process, I have identified what I believe makes an authentic teacher.

I was born to teach. I read to my younger brothers at age five. (They were one and three years old.) In junior high, I volunteered to tutor elementary kids. As a junior in high school, I became the president of the Future Teachers of America Club. There was never any doubt in my mind about becoming a teacher; the question was merely what level. I envisioned myself teaching high school English to students who would easily be engaged with good literature. That was not to happen!

So how does one become an empowered, authentic teacher? Part of the process, for me, was participating in an experimental approach to student teaching in the fall of my junior year. For one semester, nine of us student teachers moved to a small town. Unlike most of my peers in other colleges, I learned methods of teaching *while* I was student teaching. Our professors made the trip to the town once a week, and we met in a seminar to discuss everything from discipline to specific teaching strategies. We had a great deal of freedom to invent, to work together, to observe each other, and to reflect on what worked and what didn't because we lived it every day and we were there as cohorts.

For example, I organized the other English-education student teachers into a theatre group, and we presented a play to all the high school students in the auditorium. After the performance, we sat on the edge of the stage and held an open discussion about the play and its meanings. This had never been done before. The students at the school seemed to love the opportunity to immediately talk about what they had just seen with all the "actors"—their student teachers.

Another critical ingredient of that experimental teacher-education program was opportunities to directly critique the "theory" we learned in the seminars and the reality we experienced, day by day. It was truly a "hands-on" experience with plenty of room for on-the-spot, colleague-supported reflection, as well as deep self-reflection. After this semester, I spent the next year and a half frustrated that I wasn't immediately out in the teaching world. I was *so* ready for my first real teaching position!

My first big shock, however, came with that first job: teaching Remedial Reading to seventh and eighth graders in a rural agricultural town in upstate New York. My first classroom was one third of the old gymnasium that still had basketball hoops intact and climbing ropes that hung from the ceiling. (And six classes a day of pre- and early adolescents with unbelievable amounts of pent-up energy.) Two men and I shared this cavernous space with no walls between us. I had thirty desks lined up in rows, a small teacher's desk at the front of the classroom, a small blackboard, a box of prepackaged materials, and a pat on the head from the principal: "Good luck, Deary!" I hardly ever saw him again.

That first year helped me crystallize my teaching/learning philosophy. So many aspects I struggled with led to conscious decisions about what I would and wouldn't do and, most importantly, why. Those decisions formed the backbone of my teaching/learning philosophy for the next forty-three years, forty of them at two different state universities where I encountered a deeply entrenched system of rules, constraints, punishments, and dismissal. So what have I learned about being an authentic, holistic educator across those forty-three years within a "heartless system"? I learned that, as all three of us discovered, an authentic, holistic educator is fueled by the guiding principles outlined in the following themes:

- Theme 1: Seeing the unique potential in each and every student through honoring their needs, interests, and passions
- Theme 2: Observing and trusting our intuition through involving our hearts as well as our heads in moment-to-moment decision-making
- Theme 3: Evaluating our students through honoring their learning process and how they make meaning in their lives

- Theme 4: Sharing power in authentic ways through promoting risk-taking, choice-making, and collaboration

What follows are my stories reflecting these beliefs. I share them not as formulas but as springboards to creating other unique pockets of freedom.

Theme 1

Seeing the Unique Potential in Each and Every Student Through Honoring Their Needs, Interests, and Passions

In that first year, in a school that used punitive approaches to discipline, lockstep lesson plans, and standardized testing, I came to believe that truly authentic teaching must start with trust—in oneself, in one's students, in humanity, in the generative nature of life, and in the educative process. Inherent in that set of beliefs is a very clear definition of what it means to educate. According to the *Merriam-Webster Dictionary,* "educate" means:

Origin of EDUCE
Latin educere to draw out, from e- + ducere to lead
educe implies the bringing out of something potential
or latent
http://www.merriam-webster.com/dictionary/educe?-
show=0&t=1418827723

This definition lays out a clear direction for the educative process. It is *not* to "pour into" or to treat students as "blank slates." Instead, it is to see the unique potential in each and every student and to work as hard as possible to draw out that potential at all times. This is no small task, especially when trying to do that for each individual in a classroom of twenty-five students! My first year of teaching, in that gym, gave me glimpses into this educative process and into the need to trust that that potential really did exist in each and every student under my care, even though the students put up many resistances. Later in my career, college students initially came to me equally wary of a new way of "doing" school.

In that first year, in each of the six classes I had per day, I confronted a back row of seventh or eighth grade boys with their arms tightly folded across their chests, a defiant look in their eyes, and a group unity to *not* be engaged in my lesson plan or with me. I was initially floored; I had wanted to teach love of literature to fully engaged eleventh and twelfth graders, yet here I was in a huge old gym with groups of very resistant junior high (that's what they were called in the early '70s!) learners. To add to the pressure, the basketball hoops were still up, and the ropes for climbing still hung from the rafters of the gym ceiling.

What was I to do? My first move was to threaten: "If you don't, then I will…" What? I sent a few to the principal's office but learned that they spent their time having fun with the secretary. That didn't work. Besides, such a punitive approach just didn't fit me; anyone could see right through my punitive attempts and laugh, which they did!

Instead, my intuition told me that these were kids who had been ignored, dismissed by the education system, and, in many cases, ignored and dismissed by their parents as well. They were in "remedial" reading; they were the "losers" in the school. This may sound trite, but, as I really looked into the eyes of each of these boys, I saw something—a potential as a human being. I started trusting them and their potential to become more of who they really were.

One of my strategies to make this happen was to create a circle using our classroom chairs in an open space on the gym floor where we talked about any big discipline issue. I was following what I was learning from Glasser's *Schools Without Failure* (1969). He advocated getting the whole class together when there was a discipline issue so that everyone could engage in problem-solving. The circle created equality among us—no one was at the "head" of the class. I can't say that miracles took place in those circles, but I can say that they created a more trusting environment for all of us and certainly helped me be ready years later for the concept of Restorative Practices, which I shared with my undergraduate teacher-education majors. I also carried this belief with me for the rest of my teaching career: trusting that initial negative behavior masks a deep story of sadness, a sense of not being worthy or seen, but, most important of all, a true desire to actually be authentically known. What I learned from those junior high boys was to trust that, deep down, they wanted to learn and to be seen as worthy. What I needed to do was to be as patient as possible as I worked with as many ways as I could think of to engage them positively in their learning. I often did this by taking them by surprise and by creating learning opportunities that engaged them before they could shut down. I created those opportunities from a deep sense of intuition about what might draw them out to shine as learners and as people.

A powerful example of this occurred in my third year of teaching, again with junior high boys. One boy in particular was known as the most difficult eighth grader in the school. He was in my third period Remedial Reading class. My teammate and I were setting up a tutoring program between our junior high classes and the elementary school next door. We decided that Jim, from our junior high class, despite his challenging reputation, would be the best first candidate to participate in this program. We set him up with a little first-grade boy, and they met twice a week for a tutoring session. Jim was spectacular! He was mature, caring, responsible, and turned out to be intuitive. Near the end of the year, he told us that he didn't want that young boy to end up like him. Jim's life, as he revealed to us over the year, was predictably difficult. In short, he was the "man of the house" with a single mom and several small siblings. He reversed roles at school, becoming irresponsible, mischievous, and devious. Yet, we found that underneath that behavior, he really wanted to be seen and known as the person he became in his tutoring role. What we experienced was that he began to bring his tutoring persona back into the junior high. Our trust in him and our intuition that he would be a perfect match for the little boy were validated.

Theme 2

Observing and Trusting Our Intuition Through Involving Our Hearts as well as Our Heads in Moment-to-Moment Decision-Making

Early on, I came to honor my own intuitions. They are ever present, and very strong, especially in the face of a system that denies the very existence of intuition. My intuition led me to unconditionally listen to and observe my students. From the very first encounter with each student, I listened to what they expressed, both verbally and through body language. I asked questions respectfully, and I shared aspects of *my* own personal life so that students felt safe in revealing information about *their* lives as well. Such information is crucial in coming to fully understand an individual student—in his or her wholeness. It is also crucial to forming sustainable relationships that can weather discipline issues when they inevitably arise.

During that first year, eighth-grade girls made me cry—sob, actually—in front of the class at least five times. If anyone has taught this age level, you know how wonderful it can be and how cruel kids of that age can also be. I was twenty-two years old, five feet tall, with a very soft voice. I presented myself as a very easy target for eighth-grade girls. One in particular seemed to have it in for me. However, my intuition, my daily observations of her, and my belief in the potential within each student let me hang on with her through the fall and into the winter. In early spring, she came to me with tears in her eyes. She said: "My mom doesn't know how to read; I don't read well at all; and I know my children won't read either." This girl had such a low image of herself as a reader and as a person, but she trusted me enough to reveal that. After that admission, we worked together to help her change that self-perception as a learner.

Over many years of teaching in a wide variety of situations, I came to see a pattern in my planning process. I would think about what I wanted to engage students with and make a tentative lesson plan. I almost never lectured; instead, I worked to create activities that would require students to interact with each other, with me, and with the material at hand. I would gather any necessary materials, put them in what felt like some kind of logical order, and then I would let it go. Often just before I stepped into my classroom or, most importantly, often right after entering the room, when I began to feel the energy of the students, I would come up with a much better plan or at least a better order for that particular day and that particular class. I came to deeply trust my intuition and my ability to rely on these insights. They almost never let me down!

Theme 3

*Evaluating Our Students Through Honoring Their Learning
Process and How They Make Meaning in Their Lives*

Writing as a "Flinking" Process

Throughout my teaching career, I witnessed several shifts in the philosophy of writing instruction from a regimented, grammar-focused instruction to a focus on a more holistic approach—under the umbrella of Whole Language and the Writing Process—to, once again, a narrower focus on the structure and mechanics of writing: grammar, punctuation, spelling, etc. The struggles to "win" education curriculum at the national level and the connection to national, state, and local politics went a long way to help me understand these shifts. I saw the results of the turn back to regimented writing in the writing of my undergraduates in a course I taught on education in a multicultural society. They didn't like to write; they were afraid of my course, which was listed as a "writing intensive." They entered with many assumptions of my expectations for them as students and as writers. Luckily, I surprised them and challenged them to break out of the constraints they had carried from twelve or more years of "mechanical" teaching and learning and from rigid rules for being a writer. Many had learned that writing was for the teacher or college essay evaluators—an "other" who expected a certain product. I had a totally different set of expectations. I wanted them to learn (maybe for the first time) to write for themselves, to use writing to discover and uncover what they felt and knew, not what they thought I wanted.

Over many years of teaching at the undergraduate level, I developed a teaching philosophy that required students to be active, engaged learners. An important part of this philosophy was an expectation that students would learn with both their heads *and* their hearts. For many, this was initially intimidating because they had been schooled over all their previous (and current) years of education to leave the heart out—"never write in the first person!"

From the beginning, I introduced them to my term "flinking": thinking and feeling. I have come to believe that humans engage in both acts all the time and that to deny feeling means that humans cannot be whole beings.

There are many reasons for the exclusion of "feelings" in education and, indeed, in Western society as a whole. Many writers have extensively described the split in Western society between the head and the heart, thinking and feeling, and male and female. Many further assert that this has been intentional. It certainly feels so.

The writing I have always asked all of my students to do across all my years of teaching is called "personal narrative writing," which celebrates the "I," the feelings and thoughts—flinkings—of the author/student. Once a paper was handed in, I read it as if I were in conversation with the writer/student. I wrote on the paper—questions asking for clarification, supportive comments, and insights of connection—and I never gave a grade, only my own authentic response as a reader. The results of using this kind of writing have demonstrated how powerful this strategy is for creating long-term, often transformational learning.

Here are some reflections from students about their experience of personalized class writing:

- Each one of my papers was written from the heart and it was great getting the papers back with big yes's on them giving me comments on how my thought was good or how to finish my thought or even ideas on what to do in a situation. It was very helpful getting papers back that gave me tips, ideas, and encouragement for teaching, especially after working hard on my papers. It was great being able to read what you wrote and gain the ideas or even create new ones from what you said. These papers are going to be very helpful when I actually start teaching. I need inspiration, and I can turn to these papers and get the ideas I need.

- I spent a lot of time and put a lot of effort into the many papers that I wrote for this class. I tried to really think about the things we were discussing in class and to incorporate that into my writing. I really enjoyed the comments that were made on my papers, they made me further question my thinking and want to learn more.

- Some of the things that helped me the most were the open-endedness of the writing assignments and the fact that the papers were supposed to be reactions and feelings that we have about the topics that we were supposed to write about. I really hate a lot of structure in assignments and classes, so the ability to just write what I felt about a subject and tell stories, as long as it applied to the topic, really helped me to discover things about myself…to be honest I was dreading the fact that this class was writing intensive. I usually hate writing this much, but I really enjoyed writing for this class.

- I have learned that I enjoy writing so much when I just write without worrying about the structure of the writing! I absolutely love just writing about what I feel as it comes to mind instead of manipulating it all around to fit into the formal essay. I do think it important to be able to compose a good, structured essay, but I have definitely learned that class assignments can be very fun when they aren't so formal. People really write from the heart this way, rather than spend the whole time thinking, while writing, about how to make the essay perfectly smooth and organized in order to make the teacher happy. Thoughts regarding a matter in which an individual feels strongly are rarely organized, and sometimes they really just need to be written down as they are felt rather than conformed to fit something else.

I almost never directly and stridently disagreed with a student's ideas. My strategy was much more the "yes, and…" approach. I believed, over many years of doing this and many student comments at the end of the semester, that this supportive approach created the bond of trust that was essential for authentic expressive voice to appear in student papers. They had been intimidated, verbally and in writing over many years, to silence their voice. They needed much encouragement and many demonstrations that I *meant* it when I asked them to risk exposing what was in their heart. I had to be consistent in not judging them while gently helping them to question and to examine assumptions and beliefs. It was delicate business and required many long hours for each set of papers. The rewards, however, were priceless, such as this example:

Each one of my papers was from the heart and I tried to make sure that I showed that in my writing. What I have learned about myself as a writer is that when I am writing something that I truly believe in, I write better than I do when I am just trying to write a paper for a class on a subject I don't care about.

20

Theme 4

*Sharing Power in Authentic Ways Through Promoting
Risk-Taking, Choice-Making, and Collaboration*

I believe that one of the most important aspects of teaching is to consider and reconsider one's vision of power in the teaching/learning setting. For many centuries, the teacher has most often been cast in the role of authoritarian, the dominant force in the classroom. Students were to listen and respond when asked. The teacher had power over the students. A very different perspective is to share power with students. I did not give up the ability to see the big picture of the curriculum and the directions we might go; however, I also spent a lot of time figuring out where each student was in relation to curriculum goals and how best to engage each student. As described in the following section, "Weaving the Themes Together," I gave up my ultimate "power over" by having students grade themselves. This act alone greatly changed the power structure in my classes.

In that first year of teaching at the junior high school, I was required to give grades for a course on remedial reading! I intuited that any grading scheme I could create would privilege some students and disadvantage others. Over many years of teaching in institutions that required "grading," I realized that some folks take tests easily; some do not. Some love to write essays; some do not. What became increasingly clear to me was the importance of acknowledging and accommodating individual learning differences of many kinds, including personality styles, multiple intelligences, background of experiences, and a long list of other factors that create an individual learner. To honor these observations, I realized my grading process needed to take into account the many differences in all my students.

Most importantly, I knew that if I gave grades, I had power over students, and, therefore, many would not take risks as learners. I did *not* want that hierarchical power. I wanted students to feel trusted and free to speak their hearts and minds and for me to do the same. I wanted the class to be a place of safe and open conversation and dialogue. Imposing grades upon this exchange would totally change the dynamics, pushing many students back into a passive learner mode ("Just tell me what I have to do to get an A") instead of their becoming—some for the very first time ever—intrinsically motivated learners. Giving grades would create the possibility that students would believe there was a "right" answer I was looking for and many "wrong" answers, opinions, and beliefs, that would lead to much self-censoring.

Truly heartfelt exchange with the potential for personal growth and transformation would be very hard to achieve if I gave grades, thus ranking students against each other and against an arbitrary set of standards. So I created a number of alternatives over the years, finally settling on a process of self-assessment, as described in the following section.

Weaving the Themes Together
Putting These Principles into Action in a College-Level Education Course on Multiculturalism

In 2005, the college I worked in did not pass its national-accreditation visit. Specifically, we did not pass the standard on diversity. The national-accrediting body said, "You are not doing enough with diversity, so you need to ramp that up." The college's answer to this dilemma was to turn to me to create a new course that would answer this criticism. I then had the unique opportunity to create an undergraduate education course to be taken by all education majors and to do it using my four philosophical beliefs! I was not going to be censored. The college was given one year to make curricular changes. At the end of that year, the national-accrediting body would return to assess what we had done to change and decide whether or not we would finally achieve accreditation.

To begin the task of creating a course on diversity using my four philosophical beliefs, I sought out many resources on diversity education, knowing that I didn't know enough on my own to create a course that would actually affect students in the heart as well as the head. I am, by nature, curious, always asking, "Why?" and "What about...?" As I got further and further into diversity education, I became humbled by how much work there is to do to educate everyone about diversity and multiculturalism. I now see embracing diversity in all its aspects as a lifelong learning endeavor, constantly challenging my own current beliefs, being able to forgive myself when I make mistakes, learning from them, and reaching out to learn more. Creating this course confirmed my commitment to curiosity and lifelong learning.

Who Am I?

As I planned the first version of the course, I knew I believed in the goodness of human nature and the potential for all my students to come to a deeper and deeper heartfelt awareness of and embracing of inclusivity. I was realistic enough to know that individuals were on a continuum of understanding, from deep resistance to full acceptance. *Intuitively*, I knew my task was to figure out meaningful, heartfelt ways to engage all students in this journey: to never knowingly put any student at risk; to be listening with my heart to each student's responses and observing those who chose not to speak; and reading everyone's body language and watching for clues as to discomfort or resistance. I trusted my intuition to tell me when I might be losing someone, and I knew I could find a way, usually privately, to connect with that student. So, how did I start?

We began the course at the most personal level: "Who Am I?" This is a universal question, deeply relevant to each and every student, but most often purposely left out of most academic coursework. My intuition was that to start here was to create language and experiences we could use throughout the rest of the course and to create a sense of our classroom as a safe, trusting community of learners where participants could really share their authentic thoughts and feelings—*flinkings*! To do this, I knew that I also had to share my own personal experiences, wonderings, dilemmas, and questions. I could not be the "sage on the stage," or even the "guide on the side." For this course to really work, I needed to *share power* with my students—to become as vulnerable as I was asking them to be.

We started by looking at our personality styles. My intuition was that this framework gave me the ability to initially address difficult issues of diversity at a very nonthreatening level and would give me the language to use as we delved into more and more difficult topics. We looked at aspects of personality such as extraversion and introversion, realizing that—while both are valid and each contributes to a relationship, a family, and a community—our current society "privileges" extraversion over introversion, thus easing the students into future conversations about white privilege, male privilege, etc.

We next looked at the question of "Who Am I?" from multiple perspectives, including race, gender, class, and ethnicity. This led naturally into: "Who Are You? How are we alike? How are we different?" I realized that there is such power in face-to-face interaction with folks who are both similar to oneself and very different from oneself. Since I worked at a university in a very white state, there was limited diversity in my classes, but I privately asked individual students if they were comfortable sharing parts of their life story. Many students agreed to *share*, and the class became the richer for such conversations. Being at a university also meant that I could draw upon resources outside the classroom, which I did. These resource people were always folks I had developed a personal relationship with—folks I had met, worked with, listened to, and learned from in other situations.

Who Are You?

One of the most powerful cross-cultural experiences I provided each semester was a two-day session with a dear friend of mine who is a Wampanoag from Cape Cod. We met in 2004. I am descended from two people who came over on the Mayflower, and it was my friend's tribe who first met the Pilgrims. We had an instant, deep connection, and I realized that for me, personally, working with him with my students in this course was an opportunity for my students and me to learn more about our complex history with Native Americans. For those two days, we sat in a circle, listening to my friend speak about his tribe, his life, and the very real and difficult issues Native people face today. I sat among my students, participating *equally* as we listened and asked questions.

At the end of the second day, we stood in a circle, and my friend spoke to us in his language, thanking us for the opportunity to be together. Then he stepped into the circle, turned to his left, and hugged the person on his left. Then he moved to the next person and hugged that person with the first person he hugged following along behind, hugging the next person in line. Eventually, everyone in the circle hugged everyone else, just as they do in his tribe after every council meeting, and every single time we did it, no one wanted to leave that room. There was a sacredness in the air. Two seventy-five-minute sessions had created an incredibly deep, rich, cross-cultural experience that my students would never forget.

After that experience, I included a visit to the Islamic Center located just two miles off campus. Students read several articles and viewed at least one film on Islam beforehand. I understood that many knew very little about Muslims or were aware of only negative stereotypes. I'd made friends with people from the center who were on its education committee, and they graciously invited us every semester to come to the Center. We met in the mosque itself, sitting in a circle on the floor. They told us about Islam and its core beliefs. One of them read from the Koran. Sometimes our class time there coincided with noon prayers, so they invited us to sit around the edge of the mosque while they prayed. Non-Muslim students were always transformed by this opportunity.

The people who spoke to us were incredible folks. This mosque draws Muslims from all over the world. That diversity helped my students begin to understand the difference between a religion and the many cultures that practice that religion. In a seventy-five-minute class session, the speakers gently but systematically challenged so many of our stereotypes. They invited students to ask any questions—nothing was too outrageous. And if none of the students brought up the terrorist issue, the speakers brought it up. They confronted it directly: "So what do you think about Islam and terrorists?" Then they told their stories about being searched every time they flew.

As I had done with my Native American friend, I once again had the students write their personal responses in letters. Those letters revealed that a number of students were just blown away with the similarities of religious belief systems. For example, as one student stated, "I was raised Catholic, and I see so many similarities between Catholicism and Islam."

Who Are We?

For their next experiential forum, my students went to the Office of Multicultural Student Affairs where the director and I put them in small groups that included a mix of extroverts and introverts, males and females. The director asked some of her students to sign up to be facilitators. Groups of two of the Multicultural Center's student facilitators and eight of my students got together for three class sessions. The facilitators led a conversation the first day on racism, the second day on sexism, and the third day on classism.

Most of the facilitators were of color, while most of my students were white. On the first day on racism, the facilitators asked my students, "Who am I, where am I from, and, basically, what are your stereotypes? When you look at me, who do you automatically think I am?" For example, one facilitator looked African American, and she talked with no discernible accent at all. Many of my students froze and wouldn't answer because they knew that all they could respond with were stereotypes, and they didn't want to be politically incorrect. One student ventured that this young woman was African American. However, they found out that she was born in Africa and did not identify as African American but as African. A huge stereotype, "all blacks are African American," was deeply challenged in a safe, small, group setting.

The Role of Intuition in Creating this Course

As I have stated previously, much of my lesson planning in general and for this course in particular relied on intuition. I had a general idea of what I wanted to do—or, more specifically, what I wanted to engage learners in for that day—and I tossed around ideas in my mind as to just how I could make the idea(s) hands-on and concrete. So often, just before I was to "step on the stage" of my classroom, I got the intuitive idea that was just perfect for that day and for that particular group of students. This meant that most of the time, I could not give anyone else my lesson plans in advance of the actual class, which is also a big no-no in many school settings. I believe, however, that teaching is an art, and, as such, the artistry is the trusting of one's intuition. Sadly, we live in a society that denigrates intuition. All emphasis these days is on data and numbers. There seems to be no room for the ability that I believe we all have (but for many, has never been fully developed): the ability to know something beyond the world of logic and beyond the world of words. When the ability happens, it feels almost like shaking a crystal ball and having the entity of a thought or feeling emerge all at once, complete.

Authentic Assessment

The way I handled evaluation within the context of shared power was to ask students to write final reflection papers in which they reflected on:

1. Traditional parts of the class
   - Did you come (not necessarily to every class because life happens)?
   - Did you do the readings (not necessarily on time)?

28

- Did you do the assignments (not necessarily on time)?
2. Questions on growth in each of four areas of diversity
3. Attitudes toward those areas
4. Look at Part 1, Part 2, and Part 3 and give yourself a grade.
5. Discuss why you gave yourself that grade.

This task was followed by a one-to-one thirty-minute conversation with me in which they then gave themselves their final grade. The combination of writing responses to my questions and our individual follow-up, face-to-face dialogue almost always resulted in truly authentic and often difficult self-assessment.

The following class experience is a specific example of my grading philosophy in action.

Students wrote baseline papers the first week of the semester based on an open-ended framework I created on what it would look like to be an engaged learner. They then wrote up to fourteen separate papers during the course of the semester. I read and responded to each as if I were in conversation with each student. It took a tremendous amount of time on my part, but I felt it was totally worth it.

Students reported that they felt "heard" and that they did feel in conversation with me. It was a huge way for me to individualize and to truly get to know each student across all the sections I taught. Students completed midterm self-assessments using the engaged-learner framework so they knew the process and could honestly decide whether or not they were fully engaged.

At the end of the semester, they did a final written self-assessment. I then met with each student for a thirty-minute conversation about their final self-assessment document and a statement of what grade they felt they had earned in the class. This was very time-intensive but incredibly valuable. At these conferences, I got one last chance to monitor what knowledge and attitudes students were taking with them beyond the structure of the class.

Many students reported being transformed by one or another of the experiences provided in the class. If there were misconceptions, I had one more chance to challenge them. I also, throughout the semester, constantly observed and evaluated students' level of authentic engagement and their response to each topic. I was known to visit hospital rooms and to meet students on Sunday at the student union if I had concerns about their engagement. At the end of the semester, I felt that I knew each student and his or her response to course content very well. I kept a notebook of samples of written responses from each student to remind me of their progress.

Across many semesters of "grading" this way, I had many students comment that giving themselves a grade had been one of the most difficult things they had ever done as a student. Grading—sitting in judgment upon someone—*is* difficult. Since these folks would be educators and would have to engage with the grading process, I wanted them to experience firsthand the complexities of the task and, equally important, to experience an authentic alternative to traditional grading schemes. What better way than having them take the responsibility to grade themselves, using honesty, integrity, and a series of questions built upon essential questions generated by the course framework to guide their final self-assessment?

I actually witnessed a lot of students who graded themselves below what I believed they deserved. As I talked with individuals about this, I realized that they were still looking at their performance mostly in terms of surface things: Did I attend each class? Did I hand in all assignments on time?

When I asked about the quality of what they had engaged with and how much they had actually learned, many had to admit that they had learned a great deal that they were actually taking away from the class and that that was so much more important than the surface aspects of being a college student. The course encouraged students to explore and honor diversity in many ways and, in so doing, to promote greater self-awareness, empathy, and compassion.

I believe my course created many pockets of freedom for my students—spaces where they could forget about "pleasing the teacher" and instead immerse themselves in authentic learning from the heart as well as the head, learning that would last well beyond my particular course.

Part II

Lisa

"You Can Do It!"

Introduction

Narrated by Sue

Lisa Plourde sadly died at the age of fifty-six. During the last year of her life, Lisa and I were in contact while I was collecting material about her teaching experiences for this book. Lisa knew that she would never hold the book in her hands, but what mattered to her was sharing the empowerment of heart-based intuitive teaching, never a personal accolade. The following sections celebrate inspiring heart-based intuitive teaching and learning.

Three friends will be introducing Lisa: Bonnie Lyons, Emily Bracale, and Sue Haynes.

From Bonnie

I first met Lisa when she was my roommate at college, and that began a decades-long friendship until her untimely death. Lisa was immediately appealing with her confident manner, kind eyes, and gentle smile. With time I came to know a thoughtful and compassionate woman with a bit of rebel mixed in—a wonderful blend of daring and loyalty.

Lisa was a lover of literature, and she felt and understood the power of words to open the mind. Knowing the educator she became, teaching would seem to have been a natural choice for her, but it was not the career path she set out on.

Given different circumstances, she would have worked to establish herself as a poet.

An influential teacher combined with the death of her father at an early age, I think, lay beneath her decision to become a teacher of children. A career she initially chose with some reservation became an essential part of her life when she saw the impact she could have, especially with children who needed support and validation from an adult. What some mistook as naiveté was her willingness to ignore the backstory of children who came into her classroom. She understood the conflicts of children at that vulnerable age, and she gave great thought to the structure of her classroom. It needed to be a space without fear, and she worked to maintain it as a protected and safe space. She had few rules, but one was absolute: be respectful to others. After Lisa's death, I heard from some of her former students and was struck by how powerfully Lisa had affected their lives—not just to become good learners but to become good people. We should all wish for that.

From Emily

I first connected with Lisa when she was teaching seventh grade. (Lisa first taught seventh and then fifth.) As a student teacher in a sixth-grade classroom the year before, I had the children send haiku poems they wrote to an old man I'd met in Japan as part of a pen pal project. His reply came to them in the fall of the new academic year—a very loving letter of how grateful he was to receive their beautiful poems. I took his response to my former students, now in Lisa's classroom.

Lisa received me with open arms and a wide-open heart, and thus began our wonderful collegial journey. Her feedback became key when I got my first full-time teaching job in a one-room schoolhouse on a small Maine island the next year. I was there for two years and met with Lisa a number of times. She set the tone with, "Well of course you'd teach in an authentic way; of course you'd support your learners' self-aware agency and recognize them as teachers in their own right." Later on, when I heard about Lisa's courage of conviction in the face of criticism from some colleagues and the administration, I realized Lisa was like the lead goose out in front of me in the V, reducing resistance so that it was easier for new teachers like to me to fly high. Her celebration of steadfastly following one's intuition then and for years to come made me feel safe to teach from my heartfelt intuitive guidance.

Following teaching in the one-room schoolhouse, I was invited to take the place of the art teacher on maternity leave in Lisa's middle school. It was an all-consuming but rewarding time. And Lisa was totally there for me. Sometimes she would come visit my classroom, or we would meet after school and take walks together. Lisa was so kind to me and *so* affirming. No matter what I was "expected" to teach, Lisa would say over and over, "Of course the way you are teaching is appropriate; go for it. Do what feels creative and meaningful to you." Her generosity of spirit was enormous.

Lisa was extraordinary with her students. She would never "see" a *troubling child,* but instead might see a *troubled child.* She could see through to her students' souls—see what was hurting, what was lost, what needed comforting. And the curriculum was almost beside the point: "I'll pretend I'm your English teacher, and you pretend you're my student, but really I'm here to witness and support your creativity and authenticity."

Lisa loved poetry. She shared her own vulnerable, poetic self with her students, and they could feel her aliveness, her immediate creativity, and her loving connection to what she cared about. She revealed what most teachers try to cover up while they are playing the role of the adult who is more mature or more sophisticated or more in control with power over the students. Lisa took those boundaries right down and stayed in her authenticity.

Lisa's strength of presence in remaining true to her purpose—to offer the best possible experience to each child she taught, seeing in them their essence of innocence and true potential—inspired and sustained me. I felt supported and held within her ripples of light and joy to stay true to my intuition, true to my heart.

From Sue

I knew Lisa Plourde as a colleague and a friend when Lisa was the seventh grade teacher for my sons, Adam and Matt. She was a shining light in their educational journey. Both boys flourished as writers in her class, exploring their unique voices while feeling heard and honored. When Adam got his first teaching job in a small alternative classroom (consisting of all the students who had been expelled from the high school), he told me, "I thought about what Ms. Plourde would have done." He wanted to create a classroom in which freedom spaces encouraged his marginalized students to explore their personal interests, discover their talents, and strengthen their personal voices.

The following vignettes from my interviews with Lisa over a few years and my observations in her classroom during one academic year illustrate Lisa's dedication to empowering her students in all ways possible through creating pockets of freedom to invite forth their unique personhood.

Theme 1

Seeing the Unique Potential in Each and Every Student Through
Honoring Their Needs, Interests, and Passions

"Stopping to Smell the Roses"

As I walked into Lisa's classroom on a grey November day, she was launching her afternoon homeroom period with "Stopping to Smell the Roses." The children were relaxed and engaged in a room which invited personal comfort and exploration. Three tables arranged in a rectangle were in the center of the classroom, one of which was covered in butcher-block paper for doodling. Art supplies and snacks were readily available. Comfortable furniture for stretching out and comfy corners for curling up with a book graced the periphery.

Lisa explained to me that "Stopping to Smell the Roses" was an open-ended-choice time for the students to work on self-selected projects, a time out from the regular curriculum to engage with what called to them. This was a freedom space in which each student's interests and passions were validated in their own experiencing.

At the end of this period, Lisa invited them to share, calling on everyone. Here are some of her questions and comments at the conclusion.

- A boy showed a Mustang replica. Lisa asked, "What would it be like if you could shrink...?"
- An artistically talented girl shared her origami. Lisa commented, "They just have to come out on paper." Lisa invited the girl to pass it around if she felt it was safe. (She did.)
- A boy shared an abstract drawing. Lisa asked him, "How

does it make you feel?" "How did you choose it?" and, "I'm glad you put your name on it; that's important!"

- A girl shared her picture of a gecko with a big smile. She said that she drew it because she couldn't bring her pet gecko in. Lisa asked, "Is your gecko as happy as that gecko?"

The children listened to each other with respect. "They honored their classmates as they have been honored by their teacher," I thought.

"Picture Yourself on the Back of a Cereal Box. What Would You Write on the Box?"

After "Stopping to Smell the Roses," Lisa transitioned her class into their literature studies, today listening to the audiobook *Tuck Everlasting* (Babbitt 1975). Lisa invited the children to get what they needed—paper, pencils, markers, etc.—before she began the recording, so that they could continue to quietly work on self-selected projects as they listened. I marveled at how Lisa honored the children's various needs for tactile stimulation and creative exploration to complement their listening focus. One boy strung beads and did twirling experiments. There were many absorbed artists. One child quietly played with his matchbox car. The children were also allowed to eat snacks as they wished, and they had a choice of where to sit or lie with an availability of pillows and stuffed animals. I felt an atmosphere of contented absorption.

While listening to the selection for the day, Lisa employed her usual open-ended questions to draw out her students' experiences, questions which encouraged their personal connections. Lisa asked, "What is Miles's philosophy?" Then,

How many of you have had a similar thought—that you're here and you want to help the world? A dream—something you might want to do with your life. Picture yourself on the back of a cereal box. What is your goal? What would you write on the box?

"You're All Explorers."

As I settled into a chair on my January visit to Lisa's classroom, the children were sharing their reports about the explorers each had chosen to research. They listened respectfully to each other while, as usual, they were also immersed in self-selected projects. Lisa asked, "Think about all the qualities these explorers have in common."

Some answers from her students:
- ambition
- determination

- power to believe
- curiosity
- courage
- bravery
- a feeling to explore

"You're all explorers!" Lisa said. "How many of you have taken time to explore a beach?"

This launched a discussion about places the children had explored, showcasing their personal experiences along with those of the researched explorers. I marveled at the many ways Lisa demonstrated that the lives of her students mattered!

Poetry from the Heart
Audio Poetry Unit
From an interview with Rick Barter

"I've Never Seen Kids Write the Kind of Poetry They Wrote in Lisa's Class."

Each year Lisa conducted a remarkable Audio Poetry Unit in collaboration with her colleague, Rick Barter, the technology teacher in Lisa's middle school. When I asked Lisa for details about the unit, she suggested that I interview Rick. I did! The following description of their Audio Poetry Unit exemplifies the honoring of each student's interests and passions, empowering their unique voices.

Rick told me that when he and Lisa first started the audio poetry unit, they just wanted to do a coffee-table book of poetry. But, when he started having access to some cool technological capabilities, Rick suggested, "How about we try doing something a little more?" It became fairly easy, he told me, to start having the kids record their voices and also compose music to accompany their poems.

Rick believed that a poem is meant to be read aloud. He had always been a fan of ballads, appreciating how the music enhanced the poetry. "For example," he told me, "if the music is in a minor key, it can give it a flavor that's very different than if it's in a major key." Rick thought that if the students had an idea of what their poem was supposed to convey, and they picked out the music that would enhance that, and if, on top of that, they read it in a certain way—"Wow!"

Rick reflected,

So much of language arts ends up being only about the written word. Very little of it taught in school is actually the range of functional language we use. So, by doing these further steps and by having their poems actually performed by the kids, a wide range of language arts could be tapped. And it makes it more than words on a piece of paper that you bring home and stick on the refrigerator behind a magnet. It's something you can listen to over and over. I get feedback from the parents that they think it is amazing and incredible what these kids can do.

Rick told me that his part in the Audio Poetry Unit was to show the kids how to use Garage Band, the application for recording. He explained,

It's a neat application in that it's kind of like a language—little bits of music that you put together, like words of music you put together into sentences. The kids can put down a base line and a drum line, and, depending upon what kind of music they want, they can choose anything from quiet piano, violin, or guitar music to fairly raucous music—all based on what they want it to feel like.

The kids had an opportunity to think of musical expression in terms of poetry. They come up with the music, and then they record their poems along with the music they've created.

That's a significant learning experience to record your voice on top of the music to make the whole piece work and to learn that what's important is that your voice needs to be on top. It was such a nice combination of expression: art, literacy, and technology, bringing all that together into a really cool thing.

Rick went on to say that he shared this unit with a consultant who was teaching teachers how to use technology, and the consultant said he would use a CD of the students' audio poetry on his website as an example. "So it's gone around the world, and we tell the kids that."

Rick explained that Lisa's part was to create a poetry-writing workshop. "I've never before seen kids write the kind of poetry they wrote in Lisa's class—very unstructured. In the process of that unit, they read lots and lots of poems, and then they wrote their own. It's not the kind of poetry like, for example, 'Now we're going to do an exercise where you write "mother" and write a line for each letter in the word.' That's not poetry. That's a gimmick, not the soul of poetry. These kids wrote about their feelings, and sometimes I would think, 'How can a fifth-grade kid be writing this stuff? How can they have had the experience to write those words?' Some were truly amazing. Lisa had that special something to bring it out."

Theme 2

Observing and Trusting Our Intuition Through Involving Our Hearts as well as Our Heads in Moment-to-Moment Decision-Making

"I Always Felt a Very Different Feeling Walking into Lisa's Classroom."
From an interview with Rick Barter

Lisa's planning clearly involved her heart as well as her head. She was always flexible, with her curriculum, opening space for her intuitive ideas.

Rick shared that he always felt a very different feeling walking into Lisa's classroom. He described the room: the central table with a big piece of drawing paper on it that kids could draw on anytime, the popcorn machine, toast ("Always stuff to eat," he said), and comfy chairs scattered about. He always observed happy kids doing many productive things. "And they always wanted to share what they were doing with me. Many times, Lisa sent a kid down to my room with a poem or a story she knew I would enjoy." Rick told me that Lisa was always helping them find an audience.

Rick proclaimed that Lisa realized what was important and what might not be so important. "If something important came up, she was more than willing to drop whatever she was doing and say, 'Let's do that.'" Rick told me the following story as an example:

> An ed tech passed away. He was a wonderful guy. The day after we learned he had died, Lisa's kids came to me, and they said they wanted to write a song for him. (I had done songwriting with them before.) "Okay," I said. "We need somebody who will take notes on the board as we troll out ideas. What do you remember about him?" We put all their ideas together and worked out a tune. When I went home that night, I recorded myself singing the song to the music on my guitar. I brought this in, and they sang with that recording as I backed off with my own voice.

Rick related that he and the children recorded their singing and played it at the ed tech's memorial service. "Everyone was in tears," he said. Rick reflected, "Lisa believed that what the kids created was much more important than a grammar lesson or anything else she had planned for that time, and this was so meaningful for the kids." Rick asserted that this was indeed a learning experience, no doubt about it, one that he was sure those kids would remember. "It was so empowering for them to create it and send it out."

Engendering Compassion
From an interview with Lisa

You can't teach students compassion, but you can give them an environment in which they can experience it. You can take them out into the field. For thirteen years, I took seventh and eighth graders to a local nursing home. It was always a bittersweet experience. Kids experienced the ill health of their friends and sometimes the dying and the death of their friends, but they also experienced the cheer and the warmth of true bonding. When I switched to teaching fifth graders, I thought, "Great! Fifth graders, age ten, it will be just as beautiful." But I was told by the administration that it wasn't "age appropriate." I did it anyway!

The following piece is from an "age inappropriate" student:

Bound by a Wheel Chair

When I see you lying there bound by a wheel chair, I can't help but wonder why. It's so hard for me not to cry to see a friend suffering and bound by a wheelchair. Sometimes I turn to God and say, "If she could just live one more day, I would love her more than ever before," but now you have passed away it is clear to see that you and I will never be apart from one another deep inside.

—Brandy Smith

I talked with my students about human rights, followed by animal rights and earth rights. After we shared common vocabulary and thoughts about these issues, I showed the students the documentary about Jane Goodall, *Reason for Hope*. It touched them completely. I gave them the opportunity to join Roots & Shoots, the organization Jane started in Tanzania in 1991. It is now in fifty countries. Roots & Shoots encourages young people from all around the world to make the environment a better place for animals and humans alike.

One of my students got a letter from Jane Goodall! This student had been really inspired by Jane's Roots & Shoots program and had done a report on her for our Explorers Unit. I suggested that she send her report along with her thoughts and feelings about the program to Jane. She did and included a really nice letter about what she felt about Jane's work for the past forty years. Jane wrote back to her on beautiful stationery telling her about how important it is for all of us to have a reason to hope and to be part of projects like Roots & Shoots. When I saw my student come into the classroom with her letter, I got goosebumps!

In the 1999 television documentary *Jane Goodall: Reason for Hope*, Jane talked about carrying pieces of hope with her—for her, a piece of the Berlin Wall and the leaf from a tree in Hiroshima. After we saw the film, I invited the children to share their own pieces of hope: a shell from a vacation, etc. It was important for them to realize that adults have these symbolic pieces as well!

There is a part in the documentary where chimpanzees are gazing at a beautiful waterfall with great pleasure. After watching for a while, the chimps do dances of celebration. I always paused before I showed that scene, and I asked the children, "How many of you living on our beautiful Maine island visit a favorite spot, are so excited you have butterflies, and maybe dance. Then maybe at the end of the day, when you're a bit tired, you might sit back and listen to a loon or watch the waves come in?" And, of course, they all put their hands up. Then I said, "Just watch these primates and see if you see a similarity with your own experiences." And they all saw that similarity.

I showed the kids the PBS special on KoKo, the chimp, to stimulate discussion about the importance of language and how it's not just our species. And how, perhaps, if we tried harder, we could communicate with other species. There is a scene in the special where KoKo's friend witnessed his mother's death of decapitation by poachers. And he was able to not only communicate the story through the sign language he had learned from KoKo, but he was able to express his deep sadness. By seeing that, the students realized that sadness is not just a human expression. I mentioned the experience to some of my colleagues in case they wanted to show the program to their students and discuss language and the interconnectedness of all beings, and they were horrified that I showed it! But no one in my classroom had been horrified. They felt empathy.

I had a book in the classroom about a young Canadian child-rights activist Craig Kielburger, who, when he was in the sixth grade, started Free the Children. He was the type of boy who didn't ask his parents, "May I go down to the store and get an ice cream?" He asked, "May I go to India and interview the children, so the rest of the world can know what they are experiencing?" I taped an interview of him on *Oprah,* a program whose theme was "Making a Difference," and showed it to the children. When they realized that this young man started thinking this way in the sixth grade and started a group at his Canadian school which spread and spread and spread, I didn't have to say anything more. The students automatically said, "Well, we can do something." And I didn't have to give them ideas for possible projects. Each year students came up with different ideas. One year they raised money for an elephant sanctuary in Tennessee. They have also raised money for an awareness about Roots & Shoots, the local SPCA, and a multitude of other wonderful organizations. You don't teach that kind of commitment. That would be artificial. Sharing inspiration from my core is what touches theirs.

Whimsy and Play: The Puff Phenomenon

The following anecdote is from my February observation in Lisa's fifth grade class. On this visit, I delighted in witnessing a playful phenomenon that had pervaded her homeroom. This piece illustrates how Lisa jumped at an opportunity to support her students' self-initiated creative play, intuitively feeling that the process was rich in potential for supporting student agency.

Lisa filled me in with some background. One of the boys in her class brought in a Puffle. (Puffles are small furry stuffed creatures native to the online site of Club Penguin Island.) His classmates were entranced. He adopted the role of supplier and grew a brisk business. Soon there were "Puffs" all over the classroom.

In their other classes (the children had science and math with two other fifth-grade teachers in the morning), their teachers insisted that the Puffs go into animal day care. However, Lisa was open and curious. She saw the empowerment opportunities for high-interest social interactions through the medium of the Puffs. Lisa predicted that the Puffs might become an extension of each child's personality—like a puppet— inspiring interpersonal relating in comfortable, creatively expressive ways and stimulating growth in self-awareness.

The Puffs were allowed to come out at the end of the day during Free Choice Time. The Puffs were also allowed out during audiobook time (as long as the children were quiet and listened). During this day's audiobook, *The Secret Garden* (Burnett 1911), I saw two boys combing their Puffs' hair. As usual, a lively discussion ensued, stimulated by Lisa's open-ended, personalizing questions:

- Why do you think that so many people want gardens?
- Why do you think the robin is trying to befriend Mary?
- How many of you have been frightened by a noise in the night?
- What are different kinds of gardens?

Some answers: rock, sand, rose, and meditation gardens

Lisa suggested they might want to make their own miniature gardens or join together to design a garden, maybe including their Puffs.

At Free Choice Time, all the Puffs came out. Some Puffs were sporting knit hats made by parents, and some children were making paper hats for their Puffs. One girl showed me her original cartoon drawings of Puff characters:

- Writer
- Sleepy
- Famous
- Rich
- Babysitter
- Zookeeper

Lisa told me that one of her students had built a home for his Puff out of a large box, and his grandmother had made furniture for it. Lisa reported that he became a leader with this project, inspiring others and being noticed and heard in a way he had not experienced heretofore. I saw an excited group working together on a two-story house for their Puffs.

Some of her colleagues, Lisa said, warned her that allowing this play in the classroom would undermine preparing the children for the next grades. However, in her classroom, *her* focus was to honor each of her students' full personhood development, so that they might live and learn from self-agency.

Lisa intuited that creative play with the Puffs would provide a rich forum for personal and interpersonal growth. Rather than banning the Puffs from her classroom, she enthusiastically picked up on this serendipitous opportunity, carving out freedom spaces for delightful creative explorations.

Theme 3

Evaluating Our Students Through Honoring Their Learning Process and How They Make Meaning in Their Lives

Lisa saw writing as a wonderful forum for honoring how her students made meaning in their life. She celebrated rather than evaluated their writing.

On the Teaching of Writing
by Lisa

You can't teach writing. Yes, you give the mini-lessons on spelling, grammar, punctuation, etc. However, in our Writer's Workshop, my focus was on promoting student ownership of their writing process; I supported exploration of *their* personal voices. Because my students felt honored, they felt a freedom to risk-take. It was an environment in which student writing just happened. It's like taking children to the beach: you don't have to teach them how to explore; it just happens. And I think that some colleagues felt like that's not teaching. But when I gave my students freedom spaces for exploration and support for their process, fantastic pieces emerged. Here is one:

Dear Life
by Carol Zhang

Dear Life,
You hold us in your delicate love, you wrap us with something nothing can buy. You let us have happiness, you let us have sorrow. You know that sorrow cannot be helped. You know that tears are something we have to ease our sorrow. Those salted tears that flow down are made of sweet sorrow, for sorrow is sweeter than

sugar. You talk quietly to us with no sound. You help build our growing bodies at night, you help us run and play.

We must offer to help you, to help you help us live. You cannot be seen and are forgotten often. But even in grief and sadness, we can always turn to you, know that you are always there. You are in the crystal seas, the frisky animals. You are in the tall and small plants, even in the so-called lifeless pebbles. For pebbles have great beauty that is alive.

We know that your silver strands of delicate thread will always hold us, for infinity. When we are gone, you still hold us. Life is with us as we die. It becomes a spirit and holds to us. And all of us will live forever, never to be gone. For you still live in our hearts, long after we have passed away. I thank you for living in me.

"Can You Think of a Time When You Had to Struggle?"

Based upon my September observation in Lisa's fifth grade classroom, I marveled about the ways Lisa consistently encouraged her students to make personal connections between their lives and the unit of study.

When I entered Lisa's classroom early in the school year, she and the children were launching into audiobook time. She devised a puzzle for me to guess what book they were listening to by inviting the children to contribute one word each to describe the book. Response was enthusiastic: island, blue, elephant seals, dolphins, wild dogs, canoe.

I was able to guess: *Island of the Blue Dolphins* (O'Dell 1960).

Lisa passed around a bird's nest and asked, "Why do you think the girl took the baby birds? And why do you think the author goes on and on about her efforts to capture the devilfish?"

One student responded, "To build suspense."

Lisa asked, "Can you think of a time when you had to struggle to do something? Take a minute to connect with your feelings. Then find a partner and share."

Next Lisa invited her students to list how their island home was similar to the island in the book, followed by "Who would like to share their list?" A number of students eagerly shared.

Lisa was always on the lookout for ways to encourage her students to personalize their learning. She lauded *their* meanings, *their* understandings; she saw no value in evaluating them through standardized assessments which she felt devalued their agency.

Theme 4
Sharing Power in Authentic Ways Through Promoting Risk-Taking, Choice-Making, and Collaboration

Signature Dance: A Ritual of Welcome and Belonging

In one of our interviews, Lisa talked about a ritual she created to invite her students into shared community at the beginning of the year. Lisa told me that their time together would become a collaborative journey with all the students' voices honored equally with her own.

On the first day of school, Lisa brought in a wonderful garden tub from home, filled it with paint, and put down an eight-foot length of butcher paper. She next invited the children to take their shoes and socks off. Then she talked with them about fingerprinting and how that identifies us, and that Dian Fossey used gorilla-nose prints for their identification. Then she asked the children, "How else are we identified when we are born?" And someone, Lisa said, would always come up with the fact that there is a footprint on our birth certificates.

One at a time, she and her students created a class signature piece by putting their feet into the paint followed by doing their own unique dance down the length of paper. Lisa shared that it could feel almost like walking over coals because it was very slippery and a little weird. "They got to feel that paint on their feet," she said, "and they were always very careful not to rip the paper." Lisa concluded,

At the end, when they were finished, they had a beautiful piece of art that I hung on the wall. It brought us together at the beginning of the school year. It sent the message: "We're going to be working together, and we might be doing zany things, but it's okay."

"What If You Can't Draw Like Me?"

An anecdote from my January visitation in Lisa's classroom illustrates how Lisa created pockets of freedom to promote student risk-taking by sharing her own struggles and encouraging them to feel safe to freely explore and make mistakes in the process.

As I entered Lisa's classroom, some of the children were drawing and eating (one with chopsticks!). One boy was lying on a blanket and pillows on a bench with his feet up. It was audiobook listening time. The current selection was *Where the Red Fern Grows* (Rawls 1961). Lisa invited the children to draw a picture on a postcard of a scene from the book. She asked, "What might you draw?" Some responses:

- Ann and Dan
- Raccoon
- Two brothers
- Cutting down the sycamore tree
- Grandpa's shop

Lisa then asked, "What if, like me, you can't draw very well?" She suggested an option of penciling a mountain and then coloring it in with a wash for blue sky.

Then Lisa shared a personal story about an assignment for a children's literature course she took. She told the children that all the students were required to create a written and illustrated book. To get around her drawing angst, Lisa told them that she wrote a story (titled "Round, Little and Blue") about a blueberry, Prudence, who wanted to be more than just round, little, and blue. Lisa also told them that during this process she was surprised to learn that she could draw the shape of a whale, a periwinkle, and other things, beginning with a blueberry!

"Teach the Class the Way You Like to Learn."

Lisa loved to showcase her students as experts and to create collaborative learning opportunities with plenty of personal choices within these to promote risk-taking. The following observations from my May visitation are examples.

When I entered Lisa's classroom, one child was giving a

report on a self-selected research project while the other children listened respectfully (in conjunction, as always, with being allowed to quietly pursue individual explorations). The class had voted for a change from listening to an audiobook and had liked her suggestion of doing self-selected research on topics of personal interest. Some of the topics were:

- The Heart
- Old Cars
- The Titanic (a 5-year passion of one student)
- Rodents

After each presentation, Lisa fueled discussion with open-ended questions, spurring the children on to come forth with their own questions for the presenter. Each presenter was held in the status of "the expert."

Next, the children transitioned into their class study of

the American Colonies. They were divided into three groups: Northern, Middle, and Southern. They had now arrived in the New World and were setting up their colonies. She explained to me that the class had previously conducted a brainstorming session about options for presenting their learning. They had discussed plays, movies, comic life, models, games, and talk shows. The children had the option to decide to do one project within their small group or individual projects. Lisa told them, "Teach the class the way you like to learn!"

Lisa began today's American Colonies time with watching PBS's *Colonial House*. On the show, families were selected to live a colonial lifestyle for four months on the coast of Maine. As they watched, Lisa put forth her usual provocative questions:

- "What did it show us?"
- "What did the participants have to commit to?"
- "How many of you could make it the 3 or 4 months?" (Many raised their hands.)

With their personal interest piqued, I watched the children relish the show.

Weaving the Themes Together
"The Class from Hell"

Lisa's teaching beliefs promoted self-agency no matter how difficult the group. The following vignettes confirm Lisa's successful weaving together of all four themes with a challenging class.

During a summer interview with me, Lisa told me about the upcoming fifth-grade class and the reputation they carried with them, "The Class from Hell." The principal had warned the fifth-grade teachers that they would need to "tighten the reins" on their facilitation. Undaunted, Lisa told me that she was sure she would be able to hold firm to her teaching beliefs.

"Lisa, You Have to Gut Your Room."

Lisa shared with me that the incoming class had been notorious since kindergarten, and each succeeding teacher had been thoroughly warned about them. She was told that they had difficulty focusing on learning and bickered with each other constantly. "Many," Lisa said, "carried the label of 'behavior problem.'"

The principal told her that the incoming fifth-grade students could not have the amount of stimuli she had been offering to her previous classes. The principal continued that Lisa had too much art and music; that the kites, the windsocks, the boats, and the O'Keeffe and Wyeth paintings were too much stimulation; and that she might consider putting away her art materials.

Ultimately, the principal told her that she wouldn't be able to teach this class the way she had been teaching and that the students needed to be "pinned" to their desks with seating arrangements. The principal also told her that they couldn't have the reading center or the bench and coffee table or the real living room articles.

Lisa reflected,

The students coming in had had a very difficult time in school and unfortunately were traveling with a very poor reputation. Also, 45 percent of them had specific learning needs. My question was, "Had it been difficult for the teachers because they tried to 'pin' them, or would they have been more successful giving guidelines that they and their students decided on together, giving them the best learning environment for their needs—letting them move, simply move?"

Lisa Watched and Waited

With this year's troubled class, Lisa watched and waited. She didn't do rows of desks but put tables in her traditional configuration of three sides of a rectangle with one table covered with paper for doodling. Lisa figured that if there was anything else the principal didn't like, she would tell her, "Get rid of it," like the chair, called a 'comfy chair' by the children, with wheels that looked like something from *Star Trek.*

The principal also told Lisa that the pillow and the rug area had to go. She responded,

> But it's all brand new, and I hate to waste that money, and the kids would probably really welcome a comfortable area where they could just zone out for a little bit. That's one of the favorite places to read; they like to stretch out on their tummies and enjoy reading horizontally. Please let me try it. I promise I won't have anyone over there unless I'm there as well.

Ultimately, Lisa left the paints out, feeling that it didn't seem right to have everything stripped. She told me that she just couldn't welcome her students to a new school year and have them see bare walls and that's it. "It wouldn't be *their* place."

On the first day of school, Lisa welcomed her students, asking, "How do you want your learning space to look? What's going to work; what's not going to work?" She said that they liked the pillow area and they loved the coffee table and the bench, and that the children also told her that only certain people could probably sit together on the bench because many had a history of not getting along. They understood that the doodle table was, for some, a good way to help them listen and process.

The children loved the fact that they could have snacks, especially if they forgot their own snacks. Lisa provided toast, cereal (their favorite was Fruit Loops), popcorn, and carrots, which they loved too. Lisa allowed them to take the popcorn to the cafeteria to microwave. And every day she tried to add something different. "That makes them happy, and it makes my life much easier to have happy kids! Can you imagine a child during our ten-minute snack time surrounded by class-mates eating, and he or she has nothing? Just visualize how that would draw negative attention."

During their afternoon homeroom time with her (in the morning her students had classes with the two other fifth grade teachers), her students were allowed to have snacks whenever they were hungry. "Especially if they were read-ing," she said, "there was that comfort of having a piece of toast with their book." And she said that they were pretty good about picking up!

Sometimes children came in early in the morning and had toast or cereal because they hadn't had breakfast. "I didn't mind, because it was a lovely time to meet them again and welcome them before the school day began."

In an interview months later into the school year, I asked Lisa if any initial problems had continued. She said,

The only thing that comes to my mind that didn't re-solve as the school year got going was the bickering. I think if I had assigned seats, it would have kept some of the conflicts at bay, but they still would have gotten around that, somehow. So I just kept saying, "I don't want to assign seats. I want to give you the right to sit anywhere in the room that you want to. So you're a little warm, sit near the open window. So you're a little cold, go snuggle up on the pillows." They should have that choice. Also, using the paints was an issue at first because I don't think that they had had a lot of experience with painting. While they loved using the paints for different expressions, I found that they actually didn't know how to effectively handle them; the bottles would be tipping over or spilling. They just hadn't gained the knowledge; they hadn't had those art-rich activities to explore.

"May I Have Lunch with You?"

Lisa then told me that the classroom bickering changed dramatically when the children started having lunch in her classroom, saying that it died down to nothing. Lisa described how it happened:

> A boy who had been absent for a long time came back to school and asked, "May I have lunch with you so that you can talk to me about what I've missed?" And I said, "Sure." So he joined me at lunchtime, and we didn't talk about school; he just wanted to talk with me. Someone saw that he was there and asked, "Can I come in and have lunch with you too?" And so it multiplied until I had up to a limit of eighteen children each lunch period from both my homeroom and the other two fifth grade classrooms. It wasn't the same group every day. If the group had stayed the same, people might see that as an elite, special group. So the kids rotated through.

Once the children had the opportunity to have lunch in Lisa's classroom with her, there was no arguing.

> It was about breaking bread together. They sat down like a family; they ate; I put the radio on. Their voices were quieter than those in the cafeteria. In the cafeteria you were always trying to be heard because everybody's yelling. And for not all but for most of these kids, they probably saw the cafeteria as a very unsafe area, worrying about, "Who am I going to sit with; what if I sit down next to so and so, and they get up and move?" So it gave them that comfort to eat and converse with each other without that anxiety.
>
> That comfortable spirit then extended into the

afternoon when I had my homeroom period. It just moved right in with them. In the cafeteria they might have had such a horrible lunch experience that the upset would carry through the afternoon. I'd be upset throughout the afternoon too if no one sat with me, or if someone was mean to me, or if maybe I didn't have a lunch.

Civil Rights Team: Promoting a Peaceful Environment

Lisa's trust in her students' abilities to make responsible choices played out in the middle school Civil Rights Team. The team was created and facilitated by Lisa and the guidance counselor.

Lisa gave me some background. It's a state law (Maine Civil Rights Act) to promote a peaceful school environment. Students were invited to join from grades five through eight. Lisa tried to do as much as she could to promote cross-grade connections because students didn't have that opportunity otherwise. The team met weekly.

In the beginning, Lisa and the guidance counselor announced that they were organizing a Civil Rights Team and invited anyone who was interested to come and sign up. "Some of the staff," she said, "when they saw the subsequent list, had grave concerns about whether these kids would represent our school as well as some other kids with better reputations." Lisa conjectured that they thought that maybe she should handpick the group and that maybe the current group would be labeled "misfits." "However," she said, "many of these students joined because they had been discriminated against—whether it was for their intelligence or their humor or for some other reason. So I couldn't say to them, 'No, you can't join.'"

The group worked out absolutely beautifully! The fact

that this group of students from grades five through eight was working so well together formed a model that cross-grade groups could work together in other arenas. Lisa said, "When the staff looked at them and saw their collaboration, and that they were doing a good job, that was a powerful statement!"

Lisa told me about some of their activities. They organized "Mix It Up Day," to sit and eat lunch with someone different, and a "No Name-Calling Week." They also hosted two breakfasts. The team put up anti-bullying posters in the two locker rooms that were notoriously the least safe spots in the school. They made maps of the school, filled with three colors: green is safe; yellow is "I feel a little uncomfortable"; and red is the danger zone. These maps told the other teachers a lot!

In a final reflection about her experience with the Civil Rights Team, Lisa said,

> The students in my class on the team—some of whom had been targeted as "trouble"—had an opportunity to feel the empowerment of being a leader and addressing issues like the bullying that had dogged them throughout their schooling.

Matt's Drama Classes: Performances of Skits from *Holes*

My son Matt was home for a period of time in between attending Dell'Arte International School of Physical Theatre and launching his theater career in Portland, Oregon. He asked me to inquire about opportunities for teaching theater while he was home. I contacted Lisa, and she immediately invited him to conduct a drama class with her students. "I intuitively knew," Lisa said, "that this would be a wonderful art-rich activity to empower my marginalized students."

During an interview following the drama class, Lisa celebrated this empowering experience. "Matt," she began, "was, first of all, a wonderful model of a 'good person.' That came across to the students right from the start. From the beginning, they watched and listened to him, and they wanted to learn about his talent. They wanted it for themselves." Lisa added,

> This troubled class had not had enough, if any, experiences in their education career with drama, and these drama sessions were a real awakening for them. They had been given a gift, and they realized they knew how to use that gift!

Lisa told me that Matt's premise was to teach the students some acting skills through creating self-selected scenes from their current book study, *Holes* (Sachar 1998). During his visits, he taught them how they could use their bodies to convey character, telling the story through poses, then running these together to create movement through the scene, freezing most of the body, and moving only the parts that tell a certain part of the scene.

Matt didn't use a word of dialogue; he wanted to give the kids an experience of telling stories with their bodies, and, in the process, he broke everything down into simple and fun choices.

Lisa's eyes shone as she described some of the children's experiences.

One boy who was frequently absent never missed a day when Matt was in the class! Another boy felt so much pride when he worked with Matt. When he performed with the video camera on him (a child who seldom would share about anything), he shared his entire being. And he wanted other classes to see him as well, not just his homeroom classmates. He felt that much pride in what he had done. And he absolutely had talent!

Some children felt "on the map" for the first time. There was a group of girls who one day moved into spontaneous dancing together in between practice times. I think that the experiences they had with Matt were very freeing because they were done safely in my classroom. It was applauded in there, and why should it stop?

Lisa summarized that the drama classes gave her students another way of expressing themselves and connecting with each other. "And Matt's teaching also spilled over into the children feeling confident to perform skits about scenes from *The Secret Garden* after they performed their skits from *Holes*."

Sometimes Teachers Also Have Trouble Learning

For a period of a couple of months on Friday afternoons, Lisa's students had worked with two parent volunteers who taught knitting. She said,

> They also taught in third grade so, while some of my colleagues' eyebrows were raised, they were not raised quite as high. And it was absolutely a wonderful experience to see these kids not just learn how to knit but to start knitting gifts for maybe new siblings arriving soon or knitting kitty cats to sell at the school art show to raise money for the SPCA. Also, each student knit a square, and they created a classroom blanket, so if somebody wasn't feeling well, he or she could curl up in the blanket.

Lisa told me that a wonderful part of this experience, beyond the above successes, was that every student tried patiently to teach her how to knit, and she just could not learn.

They thought I was teasing. So I told them that I can't swim under water without nose plugs; I'm a little nervous about heights; and I can't get the spatial thing of "around the corner, through the window, and around." And they finally accepted that I was being honest and truthful.

Lisa then asked the children if there were certain concepts in school that they just didn't get, and they all said "Yes." Lisa said to them,

That's exactly how I'm feeling, but I don't feel threatened because we're doing this together, and you're not pointing a finger at me saying, "Oh you can't learn this, you're stupid." So they could see that adults are also in the same arena as they find themselves.

A Boy and His Passion
"I Learned So Much from Watching Him."

During one of my interviews with Lisa during this challenging year, she told me the following fascinating story.

A lovely boy in my classroom was always building, always moving, no matter what we were doing. Even if we were eating lunch, he was always building. His classmates felt very comfortable with his building, and I learned so much about him from watching.

One day we were listening to an audio library

book—*Tuck Everlasting,* I think—and I had made the kids some popcorn so they could sit and nibble and listen. This boy was lying down on the table and eating, and then he got up and got four one-meter sticks, some masking tape, and some yarn. Meanwhile, I couldn't listen to the story because I was so interested in observing what he was doing.

I watched him erect a teepee-type structure for hoisting and then create a little pulley out of an old tape wheel. Then he put the yarn through that and attached the yarn to a coffee filter. After that, he stretched himself underneath it. I watched him hoist the coffee filter with the popcorn to the top, and whenever he wanted some, he would lower it down on his belly and take a few pieces.

Just for fun after their listening library time, Lisa purposely asked this boy more questions than anyone else and his comprehension was perfect. "That's how he was listening," she said, "by building."

The Breakfast Club: Breaking Bread Together

"The Breakfast Club was one of those intuitive ideas that just popped into my head," Lisa told me during an interview, "and I didn't even think through possible repercussions from colleagues. I just thought, 'Oh, this would be cool.'" She started the club with the guidance counselor, who was looking for ways to interact informally with the students and loved this idea. So an invitation was sent out to all students in the school, fifth through eighth grades.

Lisa described the following experiences to me, her eyes sparkling:

On Wednesday mornings before the official arrival time, we would have eggs and pancakes, toast and doughnuts, fruit and cereal available in my classroom. The kids would come in at different times, and the guidance counselor and I would mainly watch. Sometimes, I would talk with a student that I hadn't seen for two years. I could actually say, "How are you?"— not just a quick, polite interaction in the hallway. We could sit down, break bread together, have tea or hot chocolate, and I had the time to wait for a response.

My student [the builder mentioned above] who loved to design also loved to cook. We went to the hardware store together, and he picked out a thirty-six-inch grill. He took on the big responsibility of being one of the chefs; he was in charge of the griddle. He was at school at 6:30 the next morning, ready. He told

me he had gone to bed the night before at 6:00 because he thought that, if he went to bed early, tomor-
row would arrive sooner. This was when I told myself,
"Oh Lisa, this is more important than what you had
initially felt."

The grill master would grill eggs, pancakes, bacon,
or home fries. He was very good at it! Another boy
wanted to be the toast master. Someone else was in
charge of the fruit and doughnuts and another student
was in charge of the hot chocolate and tea. It all was
like a big happy family. And, from the start, there were
no discipline problems.

Because it was grades 5-8, it offered a rare opportunity for kids to form relationships across grades. We had
some siblings come, and then parents became curious.
It was intoxicating, wonderful, healthy early morning
energy. I felt saturated with all the goodness around
me. I remember the way a father's eyes looked—very
childlike. He stood there, looking around the room,
loving what was happening.

The lowest attendance to the Breakfast Club was twen-
ty-eight and the highest was forty-four. Lisa said that here
again an unusual project of hers raised a few eyebrows from
colleagues, but that she could talk about the importance of
the guidance counselor connecting informally with kids to
justify it. "If I was the only one asking to do it, I would have
been told, 'Forget it.'"

The Deeper Honoring

In an interview later that school year, Lisa declared that
we as teachers can't forget children are human beings and as

human beings they have basic needs. She said to me, "Who was I to take these basic needs away? I was always concerned that they still felt they needed to ask me to go to the bathroom. I told them, 'Just say you're going to the bathroom, just so I know where you are.'"

"It hurts me," Lisa said, "that they felt they had to ask permission for a basic function." Of course, some children tested this permission. They might have said they needed to go freshen up, then they were gone for more than a few minutes, and she realized they were not just freshening up but were in the bathroom chatting. So when they came back, she would say to them, "You know, don't take advantage of this. Don't extend your time to eight or ten minutes." That put the responsibility on them.

Lisa fostered empowerment by honoring her students' talents and by face-to-face conversations about what she was seeing. She would say to them, "You have my undivided attention, and I want to talk to you about this wonderful gift that you have. How does that make you feel?"

One day, Lisa showed her students a series of incredible cartoons done by a classmate. This student cartooned all day. Lisa said to me, "Now what was I going to tell someone that talented, 'Put your crayons away?'" The student came in early in the morning to begin to draw. "She was lit up!" Lisa said. "She grew as an artist." This student definitely connected with class study times while she drew and was also a wonderful dancer. This student sometimes asked if she could come in for recess. Lisa said it made her smile because she knew the young girl was coming in to dance. "She had that strong need."

Then Lisa told me an anecdote about another student in her class who was born without two fingers and constantly hid his hands. When the boy brought in some felt bags he had sewn at home, Lisa encouraged him to teach his classmates how to do it. He did! His confidence in this arena spilled over into other arenas. He was also on the Civil Rights Team and participated in organizing a luncheon and planning session, inviting teams from the other island schools to participate. "And this student," Lisa told me, "put on a mike and addressed the whole group of sixty-two kids with no shyness!"

Lisa then shared the following beautiful perception with me:

> I saw my students as bodies of light. At the beginning of the year I could barely see their lights. Their little lights were like a firefly's light that goes on and off, but then, when you go to try and catch it, it's not there. But you know you saw it. As the year progressed, their light was there longer, maybe more like a star. They didn't see their light at first, but after they saw it or thought about it, their light stayed on.
>
> The challenge for me with this class was to help them move through their pain and transcend it. By acknowledging their needs, their struggles, their interests, and their talents and by deeply honoring them, I strived to give them a beautiful time.

Lisa provided freedom spaces in which her students could grow in confidence, inviting their lights to shine fully.

My interviews with Lisa over this school year bring forth Lisa's amazing empowerment of this disenfranchised group of students in "The Class from Hell." Lisa saw the unique potential in each and every one of these students. She honored their needs, interests, and passions through which she fostered meaningful engagement. Lisa listened to, observed, and trusted her intuition, involving her heart as well as her head to create unique pockets of freedom for her students to grow in self-agency. Lisa evaluated her students through valuing *their* learning process, honoring how they were making meaning in their lives. And she shared power with them in authentic ways, promoting risk-taking, choice-making, and collaboration.

In the final analysis, the same themes that informed Lisa's teaching with her previous classes promoted remarkable growth in self-agency with "The Class from Hell." Following her heart, Lisa knew that this would be so despite predictions from the principal to the contrary.

Conclusion
"You Can Do It!"

The following letter to me from Lisa's former student Carol Zang exemplifies Lisa's philosophy of authentic teaching and learning. It describes the context within the pockets of freedom in which her students thrived in engaged risk-taking and the environment in which their voices were honored and encouraged.

In fifth grade, at age nine, I came up with an idea for the most elaborate poem I had written. It took me days to carefully sketch out lines of similes and metaphors on the sun and the moon, whom I personified and decorated.

At last, feeling hesitant, I showed it to Ms. Plourde. As seconds passed by, I felt the nerves shooting into my stomach. I was just about to give up on my writing skills when Ms. Plourde looked up with her trademark bright smile.

"I love it," she said. "This is great! May I keep this?" I nodded shyly and printed another copy for her and decided to write another poem. And another. And another, and more, and more, until Ms. Plourde had to create a folder labelled "Carol's Writing" on her computer desktop to contain all my ramblings.

Honestly, that poem about the sun and the moon was quite awful. It was nonsensical and unoriginal, but Ms. Plourde realized that it was my Big Question: "Could I do this?" whereas a less perceptive teacher might've simply smiled and forgot about it or pointed out the plainness of my overused similes. Ms. Plourde saw room for growth and made sure I didn't lose faith early on.

My strongest memories are of her telling the class to "just write." "Let it all out," she'd smile. Once, someone moaned, complaining that they sucked at writing. She frowned. "Everybody can write. Everybody is a good writer. Everybody has a voice that should be heard."

She drilled these thoughts into us, pushing and encouraging, never failing to praise or gently correct.

"You can do it," she would say. Ms. Plourde taught us all how to persevere, have faith, and be original. "You can do it!" she told everyone. "You are a star." She had a way of making everyone feel special.

To this day, when I look at my writing in disgust and feel like throwing it all out, I can hear her voice in my head: "You can do it!" And I can see her smile, which seemed to say she could already foresee my victory.

Part III

Sue

Teaching with Joy

Introduction

I grew up in a creative family. My father, as head of the Electrical Engineering Department at Carnegie Mellon University, modeled a new way of teaching science—visionary for his time. All his courses and those of the other professors in his department were taught through labs—not just hands-on exploratory learning, but often "Create your own problems and find your own solutions." In 1964 my father was chosen to be on ABC's *Meet the Professor* show. He was filmed at work showcasing his unusual teaching methodology. My father set the same tone for our creative development at home. We were encouraged to march to a different drummer—one of our very own making.

Later, when I worked with kids who struggled with standardized learning—and yet were clearly bright and often highly creative—I harkened back to my highly creative younger brother's struggles with status-quo schooling. When my brother, Peter, finally got to take lab courses in my father's electrical engineering department, he shone his brilliance. After all, he had been building all manner of electronic projects (radios, a Tesla coil, etc.) at home for years. Our cleaner refused to go into his bedroom for fear of sparks! Unsuccessful with standardized schooling, Peter later flourished in the real world and was lauded for his creative computer-programming skills. I interviewed Peter for my book, *Creative Mavericks: Bea-*

cons of Authentic Learning (Haynes 2007). He finished his story with the following paragraph:

> A question is, since I've been very successful, what is schooling really all about? When somebody comes up to me and tells me, "Oh no, my kid is flunking," I say, "Well, that's a concern, but the same thing happened to me, and I now make $100,000 a year as a computer programmer. Be careful about how much you panic." When you get out in the real world, you don't take tests. (p. 82)

With the models of my father and younger brother in mind, I felt a natural drive to develop freedom spaces for my students in which they could explore *their* compelling agendas rather than attempting to bend them to mine.

My teacher credentialing began with a master's degree in special education in 1969. Special education in this era was psychodynamic, all about supporting the development of the whole child. Later, in the 70s, it became behaviorist, all about remediating the child's weaknesses by prescribing quantifiable goals and objectives that left the child's agency in the dust.

Upon completing my degree, I took a job at a preschool (from 1969 to1971) teaching three- and four-year-olds and integrating some special-needs kids into my program. I was given full reign to create my own approach. Harkening back to my father's teaching methodology, I set up "labs"—sections of our two large rooms—for open exploration of a variety of building materials, puzzles, art supplies, dramatic play, music, and dance. I provided an environment in which the children were free to create their own personally inspired curriculum. And I was amazed by the depth of their engagement.

One of the two rooms was entirely devoted to dramatic

play, housing a jungle gym, large cardboard building blocks, a rocky boat, and a housekeeping corner with sink, stove, table and chairs, kitchen items, and all manner of dress-up clothes. The kids loved it! I strongly believed that, through play activities, children engaged not only in self-expression but most importantly in self-discovery. Observing the children's self-initiated imaginative play became my passion.

The other room had tables for small motor exploration, including a variety of art supplies like markers, crayons, paper, glue, collage scraps, buttons, and junk items like paper towel rolls and cardboard food trays. It also housed a water table, placed by the entrance to the dramatic playroom where children could happily experiment with water toys while watching the action next door.

In the dramatic playroom, there was also a large bin of empty milk cartons, which was there just for the delight of foot crunching. The milk cartons were an especially helpful outlet when emotions ran high. My message was that all emotions are okay, *and* safe ways would be provided for expressing them. One day, one of my moms arrived with a large bag for me. She said, "I thought about bringing you mink but decided you would appreciate these milk cartons more." I laughed. One family reported that they had their own milk-carton collection in the hallway at home for use when emotions heated up.

My three- and four-year-old classes were unconventional by traditional preschool standards, but I was given wonderful support by the supervising teachers from two colleges of education who sent me student teachers. And many parents gave me enthusiastic support as well. One parent wrote,

Sue teaches with joy. Her enthusiasm pervades the classroom, yet she avoids charismatic leadership. The class is clearly the children's, and she the facilitator.

Her concepts of the importance of free play, of a variety of creative and dramatic opportunities, and her awareness of the group process in the classroom help the children expand their own awareness and sensitivity to themselves and each other. But most important, Sue Haynes clearly loves each and every child in her room. She helps each child through their own strengths.

While teaching preschool, I developed a compelling question inspired by my experiences: "How can elementary school teaching and learning be as personally relevant and developmentally supportive as early childhood education?" This question led me many years later to acquire a master's degree in literacy, which happily was holistic in philosophy and encouraged my personal research into this topic.

In between my very satisfying first teaching experience in the preschool and getting back into teaching in 1987, I was *very* busy raising my three sons. And, low and behold, they were all creative mavericks, more compelled to follow their own drummers than the school's. My oldest son, Michael, and youngest son, Matt, particularly struggled with and resisted the school's prescribed curriculums.

Michael, obviously very bright, was put into remedial reading in first grade. He failed to get the gist of how studying vowel sounds had anything to do with making sense of print. Michael would say over and over again as we read at home, "This doesn't make any sense!" And, indeed, the texts in his reading program were nonsensical (example from the SRA Reading Series's *A Pig Can Jig*: "A cat can pat. The fat cat sat. Pat! Pat! Pat!"). However, in third grade his reading finally took off when he became inspired by and determined to read *Mad Magazine*, a satirical match for his own highly developed humorous wit. Michael progressed in reading rapidly when his strong desire to make sense released him from adherence to the controlled vocabulary of his reading instruction. He exclaimed to me one day, "I can read a word I've never seen before!" He had unleashed his natural language prediction into reading his beloved *Mad Magazine.*

My son Matt's struggle began with kindergarten—all those worksheets—so I switched him to a Montessori preschool, which gave him some much-needed freedom space. First and second grades were flexible enough to allow Matt to find his own way; however, I could see that his upcoming third-grade language-arts curriculum was a mismatch for his self-directed reading and writing explorations. So I homeschooled him.

I gave Matt freedom space at home to continue his self-satisfying literacy forays. And, quite wonderfully, home-schooling opened up a lab space as well for his self-driven artistic development. Matt spent every spare moment, in conjunction with and in between our other work together, developing his drawing skills. He pulled down picture books from our shelves to study line, expression, perspective, and shading. He intently watched "how to draw and paint" shows on public TV. One day he said to me, "When drawing works, I feel nice and sharp and get that tingling feeling." That's the elegance of learning hooked up to one's internal agenda!

Fast-forward to acquiring my master's degree in literacy in the mid-1980s, propelled by my compelling questions: (1) How can elementary school teaching and learning be as personally relevant and developmentally supportive as early childhood education? and (2) How can teachers support learner agency throughout all the grades including junior high, high school, and college?

And here is where I had the good fortune to hook up with

Phyl Brazee. I had heard about Phyl (newly arrived at the university) from a fellow grad student who said to me, "You have to meet this teacher! She's the real thing!"

I had become stalled in my studies because I was told I needed to take a prerequisite basic-reading course in order to take Phyl's course in remedial reading (which was actually *not* about remediation but about the holistic approach to language arts I had been seeking). The basic-reading course was only taught at eight in the morning Monday through Friday. Well, I lived over an hour away, so eight o'clock was not going to happen. And, I also could not attend the university five days a week because of other obligations. I decided to ask for a meeting with Phyl. I told her that I *really* wanted to take her course, that I could not manage the time commitment of the prerequisite, and that I would read any book she suggested to get up to speed. Without any hesitation Phyl said, "Yes, you can take my course."

Phyl became my mentor for the rest of my master's degree program. She released me into honoring my intuition as I explored personal interests within both her literacy courses, as well as a number of independent studies. Phyl taught within the teaching paradigm of a holistic philosophy (at that time called Whole Language—see https://ncte.org/groups/lla/beliefs/ for a summary of Whole Language beliefs), which promoted self-directed learner empowerment, and this included we, her graduate students, as well as the students we would be teaching. For the first time in my education career, I felt encouraged to pursue what felt passionately relevant for me.

After completing my master's degree in literacy, I joyfully lived the answer of how to give my students of all ages the freedom space to explore self-empowerment, just as I had done with my preschoolers. The following stories share how

I created pockets of freedom in a variety of teaching forums, supporting my learners to claim their agency.

Theme 1

Seeing the Unique Potential in Each and Every Student Through Honoring Their Needs, Interests, and Passions

Education Instructor at a Private Alternative College

In 1991, I was invited to temporarily fill in for a position in the Teacher Education Program at our local alternative college. I was there for five and a half wonderful, fulfilling years. I was hired as an adjunct instructor to teach elementary curriculum courses and supervise student teachers. Later, I also taught a course in exceptionalities that was required for teacher certification. I loved it! I had just finished two years of teaching all-day kindergarten at a public school (an hour from home), so the small classes and relaxed environment of a college was a wonderful change.

The college, offering a degree in Human Ecology, purported to honor the students' interests and creative endeavors. Even so, there were some college standards that felt inhibiting to some of my students. From the beginning, I strived to support my students' agency through offering pockets of freedom in each and every class together as shown in the following experiences.

The Focus Is on Engagement, and My Goal for You Is to Strengthen Your Intuition

Following Phyl's modeling in my postgraduate classes, I invited my students to journal with me about their reflections on our readings, class discussions, and their practicum experiences out in the nearby schools (which presented them opportunities to work with some actual students). Like Phyl, I responded to their thoughts with positive feedback and made suggestions for other resources they might find interesting. I celebrated the students' own developing agendas within our shared curriculum studies. My goal for them was to strengthen their intuition to inform their self-directed learning. I evaluated their work based on their learning engagement. A student wrote the following observation:

> Sue's overall course plan was well developed, and every class was a testament to this. This is not to suggest, however, that she was stagnated by her course plan—quite the contrary. Sue's highly developed skills as a facilitator established a generative and inquiry-driven class that allowed for student empowerment and personal development and relevance. She was always willing to incorporate students' contributions into the overall course plan. All the classes were inspiring, energetic, and, most of all, fun.

In the beginning, I worked with the students in our assigned college classrooms. This meant that I had to cart around lots of resources, including the classroom library I kept expanding. Then I found out that I had the option to meet with them at my home, which was within walking distance of the college. Welcomed exuberantly by my black-lab-mix dog, the students would spread out in a circle in my living room. Sometimes I had a pot of soup to share, simmering on my kitchen stove. Our freedom space at my home felt more comfortable, intimate, and "natural" than the college classrooms.

"I Will Feel Enkindled"

As some of my students discovered interests they wished to pursue at greater depth beyond my courses, they asked to do independent studies with me and/or have me supervise their senior projects. For some, however, launching their senior projects posed difficulty because of the required Research Proposal Form. This form was reviewed by a college committee. My memory of some of the things that it included is: the project title, the theme, a list of resources, the procedure for researching, and a self-evaluation related to the proposed outcome. Basically, this meant that their research journey needed to be mapped out ahead of time. While I understood the accountability issue at play, I didn't see room in the proposal for an open-ended journey, one which might bring surprises and shifts of both interests and goals—room to follow one's intuitive guidance.

One of my students got stalled in the middle of her research project. When I asked her what compelling question was perking in her, she said that what now interested her was not listed on her proposal. I told her to absolutely follow what was "on" for her—otherwise the project was a sham. She did! And, I realized over time that, although the senior project proposal had to be approved by a college committee beforehand, I was the one who signed off on it. Thus, I felt fully liberated to provide freedom spaces for authentic exploration.

One of my students wrote an unusual answer in her proposal regarding the question about how she would demonstrate that she had met her goal for her project. "I will feel enkindled," she said. I loved it—sure worked for me! Not surprisingly the college committee rejected that answer. But that was only a form. Upon the completion of her senior project, in which my student felt free to research her ongoing compelling questions, she indeed felt "enkindled."

Thou Shalt Not Rush: About Spirit Space

I was so excited to see some of my students create their own pockets of freedom in their school practicums—freedom spaces in which they supported their assigned students' unique potentials. Within these pockets of freedom, they were able to honor their students' needs, interests, and passions, thereby fostering meaningful, authentic engagement.

Here is one example: a student in my Exceptionalities class gave me the beautiful term "spirit space." She wrote this term in a journal entry regarding her work with a low-literacy-level high school student who was diagnosed with attention-deficit/hyperactivity disorder (ADHD). She was initially told by the special education teachers that this student would need frequent work breaks to stay "on task." She was to be sure to schedule these at regular intervals.

My student launched this high schooler into a research project after she discovered his passion about firefighting. It just so happened that she had worked for a spell at the London Fire Department when she lived in England. She helped her student organize small pieces of writing under pictures of firefighting, which they had pasted into a scrapbook. She also wrote to the London Fire Department asking for artifacts to give to her student as a completion celebration.

In conferencing with his teachers, my student said that they were amazed by the amount of writing the ADHD student was willing to do on this project. When they asked if she had been giving him his scheduled breaks, she had to admit that they seemed to have forgotten about them! She wrote in her journal that what her student needed was spirit space to explore his passion, rather than breaks from tedious, personally irrelevant work. Years later, my student told me that her former student had fulfilled his dream of becoming employed in his community's firefighting force!

The term "spirit space" describes the time to be with one's deeply sourced passions from within. Rather than a break from work, which is not personally connective, spirit space gives time to reflect, to gestate ideas, to let go of mentalizing in order to transcend to intuitive depths of understanding. In the Spirituality in Education Conference (1997) sponsored by the Naropa University, John Taylor Gatto (who was the New York State teacher of the year in 1991 and three times the New York City teacher of the year) stated:

> Our present system of schooling alienates us so sharply from our inner genius that most of us are barred from being able ever to hear our calling.
>
> The best lives are full of contemplation, full of solitude, full of self-examination, full of private, personal attempts to engage the metaphysical mystery of existence. There must be a reason that we are called human beings and not human doings.
>
> Whenever I see a kid daydreaming in school, I'm careful never to shock the reverie out of existence. Buddha is reputed to have said, "Do nothing. Time is too precious to waste."

Theme 2
*Observing and Trusting Our Intuition Through Involving Our Hearts
as well as Our Heads in Moment-to-Moment Decision-Making*

Private Tutoring in My Home

For over thirty years, I have done private tutoring at home. Originally, I tutored in conjunction with other part-time teaching work, then, fifteen years ago, it became my full-time gig until now, in semi-retirement, I keep my hand in with just a few students. They keep lighting me up!

I have found the rewards of one-to-one tutoring to be immense. I have relished being able to fully focus on each learner's needs, interests, and learning orientation while celebrating their developing personal agendas. I have followed my intuitive leadings in all aspects of my tutoring work, from organizing our sessions to promote choice and engaged risk-taking to gathering resources that feel ripe for each learner. As inspired, intuitive ideas pop in, I have implemented them.

I have tutored in six different homes: three in Maine; one in Portland, Oregon; and two in Tucson, Arizona. (I moved west at the invitation of my sons, who reside in Portland, Los Angeles, and Tucson, respectively.) All of my tutoring spaces have sported a large, deep worktable, a wiggle chair, various pet attendants (one black-lab mix, followed by two kitties), and a plethora of resources ranging from a library of children's literature and research resources, to Sculpey clay for fashioning creations while we work together, to amazing, themed student-created games to practice skills on (like The Garfield Game, The Lord of the Rings Game, The Ocean Game, The New York City Game). A multitiered display cabinet has served to showcase student creations. One of my tutees sculpted large varieties of kitties; she chose her own display area on the windowsill in the hall entrance to the tutoring space. My tutoring environment has always broadcasted, "Creativity is celebrated here!"

Holding the Tension of the Opposites: Walking the Fine Line

Many of my highly creative learners came to me initially having been wounded from their struggle with standardized learning environments—strong on prescribed analysis, short on creative exploration—which disparaged their creative intuitive skills. Unaware of my intentions to promote *their* agendas, these wounded learners were suspicious about yet another potentially frustrating learning program. In order to seduce them into a learning environment which would promote rather than disparage their need for agency, I became a "child whisperer." I was inspired by Nicholas Evans's book, *The Horse Whisperer* (1995), in which he says, "They could see into the creature's soul and soothe the wounds they found there. The secrets uttered softly in the ears. These men were known as the whisperers (p. 94)."

As a child whisperer, I have tapped my intuitive heart readings to inform the fine line I walk with my wounded students, understanding their woundedness while at the same time holding a safe space—a freedom space for their emergence into their beautiful potential.

My work with my student, Stefan, is a good example of this sensitive process. Stefan came to me for a reading evaluation in the summer before his fourth-grade year at a private Waldorf-inspired school. While in many ways Stefan's school honored his spirit, their wait-and-see philosophy about non-readers left him unsuccessfully struggling to read, pressured by feeling outdistanced by his classmates. He was in a snarl and needed the scaffolding of a holistic reading approach in conjunction with a revaluation of himself as a self-empowered learner.

During our initial session, Stefan spoke softly and reluctantly. I intuited that he would need tender revaluing before he felt safe to come forth. I was propelled to faithfully listen, observe, and trust my intuition, involving my heart as well as my head in moment-to-moment decision-making.

Introducing early, predictable books (first-grade level), I assessed that Stefan had absolutely no idea how to engage his language prediction to effectively process print information. His only reading strategy was to laboriously (and mostly unsuccessfully) sound out each word he got stuck on, losing all sense of and all joy in engaging with the story. He shut down easily in complete frustration. With some coaching on using prediction within the scaffolding of engaging, easily achievable predictable books, Stefan became more successful, and I was able to find a comfortable developmental reading level for him at a mid-first-grade level. It became clear to me that Stefan's language abilities were outstanding, and I looked forward to witnessing his reading growth as he began to bring these strengths into the reading process.

Stefan's mother described him as an unusually sensitive child who loved to draw and had a passionate interest in animals. In subsequent sessions I observed how his acute sensitivity, while sometimes overwhelming, also fueled his artistic ability. And I delighted in learning about his passions. I also noted that, although Stefan demonstrated a left-brain auditory-sequencing weakness, he had strong right-brain strengths as described by Howard Gardner in *Frames of Mind: The Theory of Multiple Intelligences* (1983): visual-spatial, highly intuitive, creative, and naturalist. I knew I had yet another creative maverick on my tutoring roster!

Although in despair about his reading and skittish about engaging in failure-set work, Stefan showed signs of his creative orientation in that first evaluation session. After reading, I invited Stefan to draw a picture and write about it. This worked; Stefan could lead with his artistic strength. He drew a fisherman reeling in a huge fish from a small pond. He chose to write on my computer. A condensed version of what he wrote is:

bbbbbbiiiiiiiggggggfffffffffffiiiiiiiiiiiissssssssh-
hhhhhhhhhhhiiiiiiiinnnnnnaaaaaaallllllly-
eyeyeyeddddddddllllllllppppppppppppp-
poooooooooonnnnnnndddddddhhhhhhhhhy-
yyyyyoooooooooouuuuuuuuuuuuuiiiiiiiissssssssgggggggg-
gtttttttttttttiiiiiiiiiiiiiiiiiinnnnnnnnnnnnnnnnnggggggggggggg-
ccccccccccccoooooooooaaaaaaaaaaattttttttttttttt (Big fish
in a little pond. Who is getting caught?)

His picture of a fisherman dwarfed by a huge fish showed a wonderfully expressive line, exquisite color sense, and overall integrity of composition. I also noted that Stefan chose an extremely creative way to risk writing with me by inventing his own form—freeing him from conventional critique. I delighted in the lively humor of Stefan's message and felt lit up by his unique expression and talent. The pockets of freedom I created for Stefan were imbued with my genuine appreciation of his artistry and intense interests and my unconditional honoring of his self-guided process of emergence. My learners need to *feel* honored and valued to tap their own inner guidance and unique expression, especially if they come to me feeling like a complete failure.

Although a crack in a window of revaluing opened up for us in that initial time together, Stefan took a number of sessions to trust that literacy could work for him. Much like working with someone wanting to learn to swim but who is terrified of the water, I walked a fine line with Stefan, honoring his reluctance *and* inviting him into safer, more buoyant waters. These were the waters of engaging with predictable books, which naturally encouraged him to bring his language sense into reading, and the waters of books that matched his ability level, stretching him just slightly and encouraging him to take risks a little bit at a time. If I had directly challenged Stefan's reluctance, I believe I would have lost him.

Stefan's struggle was within the tension of the opposites— the opposing forces of his fear of risk-taking and his strong desire to engage successfully and meaningfully with literacy. Inviting his artistic talent and creative thinking into our work certainly helped to soften his fears. And I needed to be acutely present to Stefan's process. I needed to remain steadfast to my faith in his natural learning abilities as I navigated through both his frustration and, at times, my own, which was sometimes triggered by his strong resistance. I needed to travel that rough road with him, holding freedom space for his breakthroughs. Although I took into account Stefan's developmental strengths and needs, I was driven neither by curriculum goals nor by deficit labels. I sustained the faith that "we all have an expert on board."

As Stefan began to trust my scaffolding for his learning process, he began to thrive on the choices I gave him. He chose which books we would read, what and how he would write, and how we would practice word skills in games. During one session, when we were playing a short vowel board game in which we would identify the word our playing piece landed on and then brainstorm another word with that same vowel sound, Stefan decided he would make his next word begin with a "b" because he had written two previous words, "set" and "gum," and SGB were the initials of his name. This is the kind of creative thinking that really enlivened Stefan's learning engagement.

Stefan's passionate interests played a critical role in his growing reading empowerment. He had a strong love of animals and a particular, almost obsessive, interest in chickens. Stefan convinced his parents to acquire some and was devoted to them. And the fact that they had chickens at his school quite endeared him to it. A literacy tutor who was hired to work with Stefan at his school suggested that he read Farley Mowat's humorous book, *Owls in the Family* (1962). I joined Stefan in a shared reading of this book. Although the reading level was way beyond where he had been working, Stefan was so captivated by the humor and the human-to-creature bond of Billy and his owls that he persevered with success! Oh, how I reveled in his risk-taking, as well as his success!

Again, all aspects of my work with Stefan were informed by intuitive guidance. From my experience, tapping intuitive guidance is the only way to promote authentic learning: learning that evolves from an honoring relationship between student and teacher, informed by the heart.

One year, after we had stopped working together, I had an opportunity to check in with Stefan's mother about his reading progress. She said that he was now spending self-initiated time reading books of his own choosing: survival stories, rescue stories, information books on birds and fish, scouting books, and books on historical events. He had recently picked out a book on the events around 9/11 while waiting for her at Borders. His mother told me she had observed him stretched out on the floor, completely absorbed, while people walked over and around him! One evening his mother asked him about his school's summer-reading list as he was glued to a book on wilderness survival. She pointed out to him that he was a lot more interested in that book than any on his summer-reading list. He replied, "That's the way I work!"

Theme 3

Evaluating Our Students Through Honoring Their Learning Process and How They Make Meaning in Their Lives

A Whole Language Kindergarten

Prior to teaching at the college, I spent two years teaching all-day kindergarten classes—at times exhausting, but wonderful and empowering for both me and my students! I set up my large classroom, which was home to seventeen children the first year and nineteen the second, much like the preschool rooms of my first job. There were tons of art materials and a junk collection for all manner of creations. There were large cardboard blocks, Legos, and dress-up clothes, etc. to invite dramatic play. There was a cozy corner for Morning Meeting, for shared reading of enlarged books, for my read-aloud sessions, and for singing, accompanied by my guitar. We often changed up the verses of the songs to suit a different theme. The three large classroom tables served for snacks, art projects, reading and writing workshops, and math and science explorations.

As my students trailed into our classroom in the morning, they flowed easily into a full hour of free play. I wanted the children to discover and explore *their* world within the day before we moved onto Morning Meeting and our other projects. Reading, writing, and science/math activities were open exploration workshops. I created scaffolding for the children's learning through observation of both their interests and their developmental stages.

Our days also included two recesses, lunch, nap time (our

least favorite, but some of the children needed to doze off), and specials: gym, art, and music. I wove a succession of themes throughout the year, supported by read-aloud sessions, shared reading of Big Books (enlarged versions of predictable children's literature), songs, and *Reading Rainbow* TV shows. And, I must say, I felt so blessed to have the full support of the school's visionary principal. She really "got" what I was all about and admired the creative forums in which engaged learning was clearly fostered.

For the most part, my kindergarteners joyfully took ownership of their learning exploration. For a few of the children, their need for choice and creative exploration was particularly intense. Because I promoted self-directed learning in my classroom, these highly creative youngsters were indeed able to find their own way into activities they would have strongly resisted had I delivered a prescribed curriculum driven by worksheets. What follows are two examples of how I created pockets of freedom for their creative exploration by valuing *their* learning process and honoring how they made meaning in their lives.

David's Freedom Year

David—a quiet, shy boy—entered kindergarten with hesitation. His mother told me that he had had a rough time in a preschool the year before. Soon David began to find his stride in self-selected activities, although he often exhibited distress during our group times. Through observing David's personal explorations, I could see that he was highly creative and understood why being asked to participate with the whole class (like Morning Meeting) was less appealing for him than the freedom to explore his own compelling agendas.

David adored Free Play. He and a buddy spent a great

deal of time constructing all kinds of play props from Legos and art supplies, including lots of fancy swords that fed into a wonderful castle unit. Although David resisted exploring concepts of print in both reading and writing, he loved drawing fairy-tale stories about knights and dragons during Writer's Workshop. I celebrated David's creations, both his appealing drawings and the stories they embodied. I honored that he was not yet ready to experiment with print.

At the end of the year, David and his family moved out of state. In October of the following school year, I received a letter from his mother. She asked me for suggestions regarding her son's struggle with school, saying that she believed my comments would be coming from a different viewpoint than that of his first-grade teacher. She wrote that his teacher was struggling to find *anything* good about David, saying that he didn't like organized games and couldn't sit still for a story. "While at home," his mom wrote, "he listened to chapter books for a half hour or longer."

David's mother wrote that his first-grade teacher hinted that he might have a learning disability or was a slow learner because directions at the top of a workbook page confused him and reading was a mystery to him. She went on to say that kindergarten had been a wonderful year for him, which she attributed to my teaching methods and attitude toward him. This had surprised her, she said, because he typically rebelled against other people's orders. She ended with a request for another copy of the article on the creatively gifted personality I had given her, which she had appreciated for the moment and then thrown out, thinking that she wouldn't need to refer to it again.

Context *does* make an essential difference for enhancing or discouraging learning for all learners, and, for the highly creative learner, especially so. David needed to be seen through a lens that recognized his creative-learning orientation. He would, I believe, have developed competently in reading through a Whole Language reading program, which would have integrated his language strengths and extensive background knowledge into learning about aspects of print. David needed to learn through his intense interests along with ample opportunity for creative expression. He needed understanding for why group situations felt intimidating, and he needed support for feeling less exposed within them.

In my year with David, I had seen what was possible for him through making school a place where he could feel comfortable and inspired to explore learning in his own creative way. I felt sad that this empowering learning environment had not continued for him.

Celebrating Robbie's Creative Thinking

Because of his struggles with math and literacy skills, Robbie's former kindergarten teacher had recommended that he repeat kindergarten, and he was placed in my class. Robbie had severe speech challenges, and, because of this, I invited him to communicate with me sometimes through his creative drawings. He soon found a comfortable place for himself in our classroom.

Robbie surprised me one day while we were doing a math unit on patterns. A traditional approach to teaching patterns would be to introduce a simple AB pattern—like black/red, black/red—and have the children go color squares black/red, black/red. Instead, I modeled the concept of patterning with a number of examples and sent the children off to explore it for themselves with a variety of materials (Unifix Cubes, beads, etc.). I invited the children to save their patterns for their classmates to try to identify. A delighted Robbie was the first to stump the class with a pattern based not on colors but on *shapes* (a string of beads with round/square, round/square)! Robbie claimed his creative ingenuity in this open-ended, exploratory activity.

Robbie surprised me again one day during a math session. I asked the children to do a button-sorting project using two cut-down milk-carton boxes. This was the only time I ever gave the children a specific assignment (what was I thinking?). I gave the instructions and sent them off. Robbie, ignoring my instructions, took his buttons, put them into one of the containers and then, combining the containers, made a shaker!

What I learned, yet again, is that children engage most authentically when they have room to explore for themselves. Robbie insisted on his right to be a self-directed learner *in all activities,* and I delighted in observing how he made personal meaning within them. The strength of his self-agency was a marvel to behold. It reminds me of the following anecdote.

During my years of teaching in a teacher-education program at the college level, Bill, a middle-school science teacher, took my course Reading and Writing in the Elementary Classroom for continuing education credits. I like the following from his essay, "The Discovery Method of Learning":

I remember my first field trip to Rocky Point, Sonora, Mexico. As a young graduate student at the University of Arizona, I was faithfully following behind our major professor and his graduate teaching assistant with a group of fellow budding ichthyologists, heading toward the famous tidal pools exposed by the equally famous (and enormous) high and low tides of the Gulf of California. We were in search of fish specimens to swell the ranks of their alcohol-floating relatives back in Tucson, Arizona.

I particularly remember a remark made by the graduate teaching assistant to our major professor as we trooped along. The professor was explaining how he would verbally expound on the various species of fish that would succumb to his rotenone poisoning and float to the surface of the tidal pools. The assistant replied that he should not tell us the names of all the fishes that we would collect but save one or two as "Christmas presents," for us (the lowly students?) to discover for ourselves. My thought at the time was, "Why not save all the fishes as Christmas presents?"

In my student-centered kindergarten, I was delighted to support Robbie's insistence that "all of the fishes" be Christmas presents!

Theme 4

Sharing Power in Authentic Ways Through Promoting Risk-Taking, Choice-Making, and Collaboration

Planning Purposeful Language-Arts Activities

My first foray into applying theory-into-practice as a holistic teacher, certified to teach special-education grades kindergarten through twelfth, was at a high school. For an academic year, I substituted for a colleague on sabbatical leave. I taught English classes to all the students who qualified for special education.

This was my first experience negotiating the world of the special education law PL 94-142, which felt like a behaviorist nightmare, antithetical to promoting learner agency. I was required to write an Independent Education Plan (IEP) for my students with *quantifiable* learning goals and objectives driven by a pre-scribed curriculum. Progress was to be documented in percen-tiles of improvement. Fortunately, I figured out how to "fudge" the IEP's requirements by substituting *process-oriented* goals and objectives. I developed flexible plans based on my ongoing ob-servations, factoring in the students' interests and strengths in order to promote personally meaningful engagement.

The director of special education gave me full rein when he saw significant improvements in my students' literacy de-velopment. I was freed to develop pockets of freedom within the structure of high school special-education classes, pro-moting students' strengths instead of focusing on remedi-ation of their assessed "weaknesses." From the start, I both invited and encouraged my students to take ownership of lit-eracy processes, interwoven within each class's theme. I shared power with them in authentic ways, promoting safe risk-tak-ing, choice-making, and collaboration.

In my small class of sophomore girls, we sat around a cir-cular table in my mini-classroom. Their literacy abilities were wide ranging. One student had never read a book on her own. I introduced book sets that we could read together out loud. We could thus share each book in an intimate way while I slipped in helpful reading strategies, scaffolding their indi-vidual levels. I chose books that had been recommended by colleagues. (After all, my last teaching gig was with four- and five-year-olds in preschool). We read and discussed books like *A Place Called Ugly* (Avi 1981), *Sweet Illusions* (Myers 1987), *Island Keeper* (Mazer 1981), and *Snowbound* (Mazer 1973), all with themes of personal growth through coping with adoles-cent problems. We also wrote about our lives through prose and poetry. The girls were engaged!

Along with the books we were reading together, I had a classroom library of books they could choose for independent reading. My student who had never read a book on her own got hooked on the *Sweet Valley High* series (Pascal 1983). While not high literature, they contained soap-opera scenarios which matched her own life experiences living in a small, self-contained, outer-island community. She begged her mom to buy her books for the first time! And she told the Pupil Evaluation Team (PET) participants at her yearly evaluation session—in her rather petulant manner—"Mrs. Haynes *made* me like reading."

Our curriculum grew organically through group collaboration. I shared authentic power with these students as I honored where their interests were taking them. One student felt safe to write stories, songs, and poems about her experiences of sexual abuse. She spearheaded the development of a resource file of information about drugs, alcohol, and sexual abuse. Launched by our group's reading of *Letters to Judy: What Kids Wish They Could Tell You* (Blume 1986), we decided to write our own advice column, inviting the student body to write to us about their problems. And we kept our identities secret, which was terrific fun! I would stealthily pick up student letters from the post box in the front office, and, after we read them, we used our research files to answer the questions. We composed the responses together, giving me an opportunity to share some editing skills. Then, each week, our newsletters with the questions and answers were posted in each high school homeroom. Our principal gave high praise to the project when he observed previously marginalized students lit up with their secret empowerment!

All of my classes were small—from a single student up to seven—so I definitely had the opportunity to get to know my students well and to adapt the course work to their needs and interests. However, not all classes took off as smoothly as the class described above. Not all my students in the beginning were eager to claim ownership of their learning. In fact, some actively resisted *any* meaningful engagement. They had honed this defense strategy throughout their schooling. By refusing to do work that felt intimidating, they protected their vulnerability—no attempt, no risk. The following anecdotes from my senior English class of three boys illustrates how I created a safe environment for risk-taking through honoring the students' vulnerabilities and sharing power in the development of our curriculum, inviting risk-taking a bit at a time.

"I Ain't Interested in Nothing."

My first huge challenge came in my English class of three senior boys. We met during fourth period—right before their lunch break. After lunch the boys were dismissed early to attend their afternoon co-op jobs. They were hungry and beyond ready to leave the building.

On the first day, I told my students that, because this was senior English, we were going to do research projects in areas of their personal interest. Richard, a tall hefty lad, pounded his fist on the table and said, "I ain't interested in nothing!" What follows is my story of how patient negotiating and radical personal honoring inspired a warm bond between Richard and me.

I don't remember what we actually did in senior English that first day; I suspect I felt completely flummoxed and more than a little anxious. I intuitively knew, however, that pushing my agenda would never work, nor did I wish to try. I hoped to spark their engagement through tapping *their* interests. So, no interests... And the other two classmates followed Richard's lead.

I knew that I first needed to convey—nonverbally—that I understood and respected Richard's defense system and all the hurt it covered up, while concurrently nudging him to take risks a little bit by little bit. In order to start *somewhere*, *I* chose the class theme, "Oceans," because we all lived on an island, one of the boys worked in a boatyard, and one felt attracted to oceanography. I planned activities like the shared reading of novels and articles related in any way to oceans. We did a bit of individual research on sea creatures and wrote a bit in response journals about the ideas we explored. In our early days together, Richard often rejected the day's agenda and suggested alternative activities, often word games like "Hangman." If we played games one class period, he would acknowledge my suggestions the following class period. As time went on, I knew that Richard was beginning to value my respect for him—he knew he couldn't push too far. And so a freedom space for risk-taking was cocreated through sharing power.

Engagement happened slowly. Further into the semester, when we shared the reading of parts of the thriller *The Deep* (Benchley 1976), the boys got into it, especially with the promise of watching the movie *The Deep* (1977), based on the book, when we finished. We all took turns reading out loud, while I gently and unobtrusively shared helpful reading strategies and confirmed their progress in using them. Introducing computerized word processing in writing (in 1987) also enticed these students into further risk-taking.

Survival Food

By the beginning of our second semester we were in a kind of flow, and I felt the boys were ready to share more power with me through cocreating the curriculum. "So," I asked the boys, "What theme shall we explore this semester?" "Food," exclaimed Richard, taking the lead again—no doubt hungry as usual during this fourth period.

So we launched a unit on survival food. We watched documentaries like *Will the World Survive?* and *Nomads of the Rain Forest* and films like *Never Cry Wolf* (1983). Integrating films worked *really* well. The students really took over, however, during our Friday cooking classes. Utilizing an electric frying pan, toaster oven, and a budget of fifty dollars, the boys planned, cooked, and served a lunch, all within forty-five minutes. "After all," one of the students quipped, "after this year, we will be out on our own; that's survival!" We were having fun!

Toward the end of the semester, we shared the reading of *Adrift: 76 Days Lost At Sea* (Callahan 1983), in which the author details his account of being stranded on a raft in the Atlantic Ocean for seventy-six days with no formal survival training. Related to our survival food unit exploration, we learned that Callahan ate every part of the fish he caught, even the fish eyes for the rich iodine. During the time of our reading, my small classroom was being moved to another small renovated room (that used to be a storage closet) down the hall. It had been freshly painted when we first moved in, and I was able to get permission to hold our class outside on nice days to avoid the fumes. In the large high school parking lot, empty of students except for us, we gathered in the back of Richard's truck, pretending it was a raft while we took turns reading *Adrift*. Reading flowed; contentment reigned. We felt a guilty pleasure being outside in this freedom space we cocreated.

In sharing power with these students, my goal was to invite them into a collaborative journey of meaningful exploration. In opening up the curriculum, I needed to be very patient about their resistance to any kind of engagement. In time, by not reacting to this resistance and by continuing to honor my students in every way possible, meaningful engagement did indeed happen!

Just a Story

One day toward the end of the school year, Richard wrote the following piece, entitled "Just a Story." He shared it with me and also said that I could share it with his classmates. He said that it was not about himself...

Just a Story

THE ONLY THING THAT I LIKE ABOUT THE SCHOOL IS THAT I GET TO LEAVE AT 12:00. THERE IS ONE MORE THING I DO LIKE, THAT IS ENGLISH CLASS. THE SCHOOL IS SO DIFFERENT. WE HAVE TO DO WHAT EVERY BODY TELLS USE TO DO. PEOPLE I HAVE NEVER TALK TO BEFORE TELL ME THAT I BETTER GO TO MY CLASS. THEY SHOULD GO AFTER THE PEOPLE THAT DO THAT STUFF. I HAVE BEEN IN ALOT OF TROUBLE IN THIS SCHOOL. THE ONLY THING ABOUT IT IS THAT PEOPLE NEVER FORGET. THE TEACHERS LOOK AT ME LIKE I SHOULD BE SOME WHERE, NOT HERE. I GET SICK OF PEOPLE SAYING STUFF ABOUT ME AND LOOKING AT ME FUNNY. THE TEACHER IS ONE OF THE THINGS THAT MAKE THING HARD FOR ME. THEY ALLWAYS NO THE BEST. THEY ARE NEVER WRONG. THE PRISCIPLE NEVER BELEAVES THE STUDENT. THEY ALLWAYS SAY THAT THEY BELEAVE THE TEACHER. I WOULD SOME DAY LIKE TO BE IN

THE HIGH SEAT FOR ONE DAY. LET THE TEACHERS
BE THE STUDENT. THEY WILL THINK ABOUT WHAT
I HAVE SAID.

My heart swelled with this evidence that Richard felt honored and safe enough to reveal his longstanding hurt. Also,
by saying, "There is one thing I do like, that is English class,"
he intimated that some elemental healing had occurred in
our class because, I believe, I shared power with the students
through honoring and implementing their ideas and their interests. I had hoped that my students would become more
comfortable reading and would feel the personal engagement
books can foster. I had hoped that they would become more
comfortable writing and bring forth their individual voices.
Well, Richard did. However tentative Richard's self-concept
as a learner remained, he had successfully tapped his "voice."
Through promoting student agency out front, through promoting risk-taking with achievable tasks within which there
were lots of choices, and through collaborating and sharing
power in creating our curriculum, I felt successful in cocreating pockets of freedom with my vulnerable students. Although
I was challenged in ways I could never have anticipated, I felt
it had been a dear and surprisingly rewarding year!

Weaving the Themes Together: A Case Study of
Christina, a Student in a Small Island School

For a number of years, during my 37 years of living on the
coast of Maine, I had the unique experience of teaching special
education on a small outer island accessed by the mailboat.
The island's elementary two-room schoolhouse hosted two
teachers and an average of thirteen children. Life for the children on this small island harkened back to the days when chil-

dren could explore freely, initiating play in multi-age groups without the need for adult vigilance or the regimentation of after-school activities. The island sang with the exuberant voices of free-ranging kids.

Due to the small size of the island's elementary school, the teachers were often able to offer special help for any student struggling with the curriculum. School was generally a happy, productive environment. I was hired as a special education teacher, however, to work with a student who, despite all efforts by her teachers, was sinking into despair over her learning struggles.

Because of both my training in Whole Language literacy and my experiences with working with a variety of highly creative students, I was able to offer my student, Christina, pockets of freedom within the standard curriculum, which inspired her to revalue herself as a competent, talented learner. We worked together for three years, fourth through sixth grade.

Supporting Christina's Creative Orientation Unlocked Engagement.

Christina's teachers told me that she had just about given up. Christina felt intense frustration with her classroom work; she felt like a complete failure as a learner. Christina's teachers knew that she was bright, despite her specific learning struggles, but they felt powerless to ease her frustration and dispel her belief that she was stupid. Even an assessment affirming her high IQ did nothing to alter her belief.

At a PET meeting following her testing, Christina was identified as "learning disabled" in the areas of reading, writing, and math. After talking with her teachers and working with Christina during our initial session, I expressed my belief that she was, in fact, not only very bright but highly creative.

Along with seeing Christina's obvious challenges with her schoolwork, I could see, on another level, Christina's highly creative orientation in all aspects of her learning. Supporting Christina's creativity gave her the freedom space within which she was able to unlock her engagement.

We worked in a small storage room in back of the two classrooms in which we carved out a workspace and made it our own. Christina loved to draw, and her pictures displayed wonderful line, perspective, color, details, and expression. She was, in fact, driven to explore themes artistically, engaging in drawing and craft work at any given opportunity. (Her intricate Sculpey Clay creations were amazing.) Her artwork decorated our learning space. I allowed Christina to draw and craft as we worked together in order to honor her talent *and* energize her focus for our task at hand. I also arranged for Christina to have an art mentorship with the teacher's aide, Gail, who is an artist. Visits to Gail's house became a highlight of her week.

I Offered Choices in All Areas of Studies.

In our work with reading, writing, and math, I gave Christina choices of the resources we used, the topics we would explore, and our formats for practice. Highly creative learners have intense need for ownership in every aspect of their learning, and their strong intuitive ability makes them excellent choice-makers. I have always been amazed to see these learners sort through a considerable pile of book choices, for example, rapidly prioritizing them into "maybe now," "at some future time," and "let go." Their intuitive tuning fork seems to know just what will work for them. Choice is a powerful "pocket of freedom" that invites learners to claim their agency.

Christina Chose Stories That Resonated with Her Deep Sensitivities and Perceptions.

The first book Christina chose for our reading work together was *The Worry Week* (Lindbergh 1985). The book is about three girls who connive to stay alone at their beloved vacation home on an island off the coast of Maine while their parents are away at a funeral. Allegra, who tells the story, is the middle sister, a similarity to Christina's middle position in her own family; she was sandwiched between an older sister and younger twin sisters.

To increase Christina's confidence in reading, I encouraged her to draw upon her rich language prediction. Only after Christina had a good idea about what kind of word *might* fit the context, did I share helpful ideas for integrating aspects of the print information. Without prediction—the gas that drives the reading process—reading can feel like an intimidating, laborious task. Christina's confidence in her reading grew as her use of *meaning-oriented* strategies brought success. As Christina became fully engaged with her reading, she showed a deep understanding of the book themes. And I rejoiced in her identification with the characters and the situations in the story.

Christina's rich bonding with stories continued through books with sophisticated themes, such as David's growth of self-identity in *North to Freedom* (Holm 1963), about the escape of a young boy from a concentration camp and his awakening from a deadened state of existence, and Cusi's journey to embrace his ordained destiny in *Secret of the Andes* (Clark 1952). These are the kinds of books Christina chose and delighted in, stories which resonated with her remarkable sensitivities and perceptions.

To encourage and support Christina's enjoyment of the

stories we read, I engaged in relaxed, spontaneous conversations with her rather than asking her to respond to specific questions. Her engagement and comments on our reading were all the evaluation I needed. Christina's deep personal connection to the stories would lead her to argue sometimes with the characters. One day while we were reading *The Secret of the Andes*, she became impatient with Cusi when he got sidetracked from his life mission, saying, "I think he should try to find out who he is rather than trying to find a family." She also commented, at this juncture in his traveling, "I miss Chuto." Chuto was Cusi's teacher, who was waiting for his return in the hidden valley of their home. Following our reading when we watched the PBS video *The Incas,* Christina transformed this rather dry documentary, exclaiming, "That's Cusi's mother's hut," and, "That's his llama, Misty." When I shared her responses with her art mentor Gail, she commented, "And for her, they really were."

Christina Set Off with Full Wind in Her Sails.

In writing, I encouraged Christina to brainstorm a story idea that would spark an "organizing vision" compelling enough to encourage her risk-taking and investment. Christina's previous attempts at writing had provoked frustration related to her challenges in spelling, punctuation, and penmanship. Christina had also found it difficult to engage with writing assignments that were not in tune with her personal interests. As a highly creative learner, Christina needed to feel relevancy.

I invited Christina to write on my portable computer to bypass her handwriting angst, and, while this novelty helped, she was still unable to find an appealing idea. In order to start *somewhere*, I suggested that she continue with a piece she had written for her school newspaper about a young Russian girl immigrating to this country in the mid-1800s. Reluctantly, she began, placing the girl in Texas. Plodding along, Christina wrote a few lines each week with many pleas for typing help.

One day, Christina had her main character escape from her chores to visit a nearby creek. At the creek, the girl saw a man. "Or was it a boy?" I suggested, jumping in with an intuitive idea. "Oh yes," she said, "a young black boy who had escaped from a cruel master." Fueled by this compelling idea, feeding her strong sense of social justice, Christina set off with full wind in her sails. "Natasha's Adventures," the story of how a young girl helped an abused slave boy connect with the Underground Railroad, became a beautifully illustrated little book. Christina's transition from repressed writer to empowered author was a delightful unfolding as she began to re-envision herself as a capable author and illustrator.

One Must Ask, "Memory in What Context?"

Christina and I still had the potential tedium of math and spelling skills to work on. Within my holistic developmental approach, I assessed where Christina had become stuck foundationally in both subjects.

In math, Christina was not using number sense in computation and thus had difficulty learning her facts. Often with identified "learning-disabled" students, this difficulty is deemed a short-term memory problem. However, it is my experience that a highly creative learner often does not retain memory for facts isolated from personal understanding or relevance. One must ask, "Memory in what context?"

For math computation work, we brainstormed card games to practice number sense. First we reviewed the "10 + any number" rule and doubles. I also had Christina develop a fluent sense of counting up and back by twos on odds and evens. Once Christina was fluent in counting by twos and had learned the "10 + any number" rule and doubles, I taught her how to quickly figure out almost any addition fact by beginning with doubles or +10 and adding or subtracting 1 or 2 as necessary (for example 9 + 7 is 10 + 7 − 1 and 8 + 6 is 6 + 6 + 2). Multiplication is multiple addition, so I encouraged Christina to go back to a fact she knew and use her addition strategies (for example, to get 8 x 7, go to 8 x 6 = 48, and then add + 10 − 2). Once you have solidly learned addition and multiplication, then subtraction and division can be figured out by reference to the former (17 − 8 turned into 8 + what? = 17).

Christina Was Quite Motivated to Practice Skills on Games *She* Created.

After I assessed Christina's developmental level in spelling, using a Features Test from *Words Their Way* (Bear 1996), we brainstormed rules and practice words drawn from the book's foundational spelling program. Christina would have rebelled against memorizing spelling features, but she was quite motivated to practice these on games she created, varying the rules to keep us on our toes.

Christina became a far more confident learner. She grew in her reading, writing, spelling, and math skills, although in spelling she still tended to go into a shorthand version when writing "on the run." Composing on a computer helped Christina focus on expressing her thoughts, bypassing her handwriting struggles. While she composed more confidently, Christina still needed that spark of inspiration to create a piece with strong voice and energy. And, while not quite as fluent a reader as a classmate she read with, Christina amazed her teacher with her depth of understanding inference, characterization, and theme.

One day, while Christina and I sat together on the mailboat which serviced her island, I noticed how absorbed she was in reading a babysitting handbook for an elective course she was taking. I smiled because I had been wondering how her independent reading was developing. At one point, she looked up at me and said, "Sometimes I really love riding on the boat, because I get to read a lot and relax."

Within our small workspace, Christina and I cocreated a freedom space within which she felt supported as a learner who had an intense need to be true to her strong interests and who *had* to employ creative initiative to effectively fuel her learning. I flew with my intuition about what might spark Christina's engagement. I assessed Christina's progress through not just skills growth but also anecdotal evidence of her enlivened self-directed learning. Most importantly, I truly valued Christina's determination to claim agency in her learning, understanding her refusal to engage with what felt like "bogus" work.

Even more than the choices I gave her or the games we created together, I feel that my *honoring of Christina* was the true catalyst for her empowerment.

Part IV

Neuroscience Support
for Teaching
from the Heart,
as well as the Head

Introduction

What follows is Phyl's search for scientific support for our beliefs. While we didn't need to feel validated by the scientific authentication of these beliefs, we found its existence heartwarming.

Neuroscientists Are Finding Out That *Both* the Left-Brain Hemisphere and the Right-Brain Hemisphere Are Necessary for Learning.

Educators and others have talked for quite awhile now about how our brain has two distinct hemispheres: (1) the left brain, which is logical, linear, computerlike, and analytical; and (2) the right brain, which sees the big picture, empathizes, recognizes patterns, draws from heart-based intuition, and creates meaning. Until recently, psychologists, scientists, and many educators believed the left brain was superior. As a result, much of our formal educational system has reflected left-brain qualities, shunning the gifts of the right brain.

What neuroscience is finding (and what many of us have always intuited) is that *both* hemispheres are necessary for learning and for life. As Daniel Pink says in his book *A Whole New Mind* (2005), the hemispheres are just different. "The left hemisphere reasons sequentially, excels at analysis, and handles words. The right hemisphere reasons holistically, recognizes patterns, and interprets emotions and nonverbal expressions. Human beings are literally of two minds (p. 14)." What he and many others are ultimately saying is that we need both. What we need to do is to learn how to assist these two hemispheres in working together for the greater good, rather than being pitted against each other, inside ourselves, between individuals. We need to value them coequally, in life and in our educative processes.

A very dramatic story about hemispheres of the brain and the power of each in one's life comes from Jill Bolte Taylor, PhD, who in her book *My Stroke of Insight* (2009) tells her story of experiencing a massive stroke in the left side of her brain. As a neuroanatomist, she observed her own mind deteriorate to the point that she could not walk, talk, read, write, or remember any of her life; the left-brain functions stopped working. At the same time, for the first time in her life, she fully came to experience her right brain, which brought her a sense of complete well-being and inner peace. After eight years of recovery, Taylor healed completely but with a deep respect for and understanding of the importance of the right brain and all it stands for. She spends much of her time these days talking to audiences about the importance of both hemispheres.

Emotional Intelligence (EQ) Is a Basic Requirement for the Effective Use of IQ.

In the early part of the twentieth century, IQ became incredibly important as the way to identify who was and who wasn't "smart." The focus was on the rational intelligence that we use to solve logical or strategic problems. However, in the mid-1990s, Daniel Goleman popularized research from many neuroscientists and psychologists showing that emotional intelligence (EQ) is of equal importance to IQ. EQ gives us our awareness of our own and other people's feelings. It gives us empathy, compassion, motivation, and the ability to respond appropriately to pain or pleasure. EQ is a basic requirement for the effective use of IQ. If the brain areas with which we feel emotions are damaged, we think less effectively. In fact, as professor Robert Sylwester stated, "We know emotion is important in education—it drives attention, which in turn drives learning and memory (par. 4)." In other words, to truly learn, one must start with emotions! This has such importance for us as authentic teachers.

Candace Pert, a psychoneuroimmunologist and author of the book *Molecules of Emotion: Why You Feel the Way You Feel* (1997), studied the connection between emotions and actual molecules in the body. She discovered that "recent technological innovations have allowed us to examine the molecular basis of the emotions, and to begin to understand how the molecules of our emotion share intimate connections with, and are indeed from, our physiology. It is the emotions, I have come to see, that link mind and body...the molecules of emotion run every system in our body...(pp. 18-19)." She agreed with Sylwester that learning is an emotional event, impacted by how we're feeling. One of her most important findings for educators was that people can't grasp new information in a state of fear and that punishment and threats actually, physically, inhibit the learning process.

We Humans Are Wired for Compassion, Altruism, and Empathy.

The implications of all this research for authentic teaching and learning are huge. The Association for Supervision and Curriculum Development (ASCD), a national education organization, created a focus on the education of the Whole

Pockets of Freedom

Child—the thinking and feeling child. Until recently, we as a society have revered the thinking brain that is logical, linear, analytical, and technical. We have structured our educational systems around it. Pert's, Taylor's, Goleman's, and many others' work is now questioning this imbalance and instead is asking us to clearly support the equivalent importance of the feeling brain—the caring, altruistic, empathic, and intuitive heartbrain.

> Most of us have been taught in school that the heart is constantly responding to "orders" sent by the brain in the form of neural signals. However, it is not as commonly known that the heart actually sends more signals to the brain than the brain sends to the heart! Moreover, these heart signals have a significant effect on brain function—influencing emotional processing as well as higher cognitive faculties such as attention, perception, memory, and problem-solving. In other words, not only does the heart respond to the brain, but the brain continuously responds to the heart. ("Scientific Foundation of the HeartMath System" from the first page of this website: https://www.heartmath.org/science)

With such scientific understanding of the physical reality of emotions, intuition, feelings, and their utmost importance in the learning process, new research is further confirming what many people have always known that we humans are wired for compassion, altruism, and empathy to be in mutually growth-enhancing relationships. Daniel Goleman, in his book on *Social Intelligence* (2006), states,

We are wired to connect. Neuroscience has discovered

126

that our brain's very desire makes it sociable, inexorably drawn into an intimate brain-to-brain linkup whenever we engage with another person. That neural bridge lets us affect the brain—and so the body—of everyone we interact with, just as they do us. (p. 4)

The implications of this for the teaching/learning process are immense. Goleman further states, "Our relationships mold not just our experience but our biology...nourishing relationships have a beneficial impact on our health, while toxic ones can act like slow poison in our bodies (p. 5)." He goes on to say, "...being chronically hurt and angered, or being emotionally nourished, by someone we spend time with daily over the course of years, can refashion our brains (p. 11)." Therefore, how teachers connect to their students has unimaginable significance. We are wired to live and learn in relationship with each other, and teachers have a unique opportunity and responsibility to make that relationship as authentic and nourishing as possible.

Work done by Shelley Taylor confirms this, and, in her book entitled *The Tending Instinct: Women, Men, and the Biology of Our Relationships* (2002), she states,

One of my goals in this book [is] to add balance to our view of human nature....I want you to recognize that the caregiving we provide to others is as fundamental to human nature as our selfishness or aggression.... We have neurocircuitries for tending as surely as we have biological circuitry for obtaining food...Scientific evidence suggests that we have been caregivers since the outset of our existence...We are fundamentally a nurturant species...The brain and body are crafted to tend, not indiscriminately so, but in order to attract, maintain, and nurture relationships with others across the life span. (p. 3)

Authentic teaching must focus on "tending" and nurturing relationships.

Flinking Is the Act of Feeling and Thinking at the Same Time.

All this scientific research brings me back to the beginning: to our centuries-old imbalance of thinking over feeling and our need to find a new balance in how we view human nature and the acts of teaching and learning. Science now confirms that we learn with both our logical brain and our intuitive feeling brain. My insights into this compelled me to create a new word to reflect this balance: "flinking," the act of feeling and thinking at the same time.

Conclusion

> We all know that what will transform education is not
> another theory, another book, or another formula but
> educators who are willing to seek a transformed way
> of being in the world. In the midst of the familiar trap-
> pings of education—competition, intellectual combat,
> obsession with a narrow range of facts, credits and cre-
> dentials—what we seek is a way of working illumined
> by spirit and infused by soul.
>
> —Parker Palmer

We, the authors, believe that increasing numbers of us are
being called to develop our fuller potential as we awaken to
an expanded understanding of our intuitive and creative abilities. Responding to this awakening, we will have the capacity
to transform our culture and the purpose of education. This
is not a time for narrowing consciousness by focusing on measurable, objective learning goals. Commitment to developing
our expanded potential and supporting growth of agency in
ourselves and others can confront and transform the reduc-
tionist mentality in education and our culture, which has so
greatly limited us.

In our book we have explored the conditions of education
transformation that foster authentic learning empowerment.
As we each presented in these pages, we three educators

worked consistently to create pockets of freedom in each of our teaching/learning settings. We did this through:

- Seeing the unique potential in each and every student through honoring their needs, interests, and passions;
- Observing, and trusting our intuition, through involving our hearts as well as our heads in moment-to-moment decision-making;
- Evaluating our students through honoring their learning process and how they make meaning in their lives; and
- Sharing power in authentic ways through promoting risk-taking, choice-making, and collaboration.

Carl Rogers writes the following about empowered learning in *Freedom to Learn for the 80's* (1983):

We know—and I will briefly mention some of the evidence—that the initiation of such learning rests not upon the teaching skills of the leader, not upon scholarly knowledge of the field, not upon curricular planning, not upon use of audiovisual aids, not upon the programmed learning used, not upon lectures and presentations, not upon an abundance of books, though each of these might at one time or another be utilized as an important resource. No, the facilitation of significant learning rests upon certain attitudinal qualities that exist in the personal *relationship* between the facilitator and the learner. (p. 121)

Teachers whose lived experience is not sourced from their intuitive knowing are unlikely to reach out to support authentic empowerment in their learners. The need to define and control learning in an objective, measurable fashion—the foundation of traditional education—stems from the philosophical life view of individuals who source their living from cultural directives alone. In *The Courage to Teach* Parker Palmer asserts, "Deep speaks to deep, and when we have not sounded our own depths, we cannot sound the depths of our students' lives (p. 31)." Individuals devoted to the call to be true to their own awakening can inspire awakening in others.

Teaching that is passionate and fully alive comes from living that is passionate and fully alive, ever expanding as empowerment grows from unlimited depths. What's missing in the education climate of the past few decades is recognition of the amazingly rich diversity of learners who need to be seen and honored for who they are in order to develop their unique potential. Recognition is also missing for the rich diversity of talented teachers who are increasingly diverted from their intuitive ability to create curriculums which support their learners' agency. Pockets of freedom for both learners and teachers are needed now more than ever! If we are truly to follow Parker Palmer's advice—to reform education from the inside out—we need teachers who are strong in themselves and strong in their commitment to accessing their heart-based intuition. We hope this book inspires educators to create their own pockets of freedom, eventually joining together to fashion a whole, beautiful garment of freedom, inspiration, vibrancy, love, and lifelong learning.

Bibliography

Gardner, Howard. *Frames of Mind: The Theory of Multiple Intelligences*. New York: Basic Books, 1983.

Glasser, William. *Schools Without Failure*. New York: Harper & Row, 1969.

Goleman, Daniel. *Emotional Intelligence*. New York: Penguin Random House, 2005.

———. *Social Intelligence: The New Science of Human Relationships*. New York: Bantam Dell, 2006.

Grauer, Stuart. *Fearless Teaching*. New York: Alternative Education Resource Organization (AERO), 2016. Quoted, with permission, from the chapter, "In Praise of Hooky."

Haynes, Sue. *Creative Mavericks: Beacons of Authentic Learning*. Bloomington, IN: Xlibris Corporation, 2007.

Merriam–Webster, Inc., accessed in 2009. http://merriam-webster.com/dictionary/educe?show=0&t=1418827723.

Palmer, P. J. *The Courage to Teach: Exploring the Inner Landscape of a Teacher's Life*. San Francisco: Jessie-Bass Publishers, 1998.

Pert, Candace. *Molecules of Emotion: Why You Feel the Way You Feel*. New York: Scribner, 1997.

Pink, Daniel. *A Whole New Mind*. New York: Riverhead Books, 2005.

Rajvanshi, Anil K. "The three minds of the body—Brain, heart and gut," in Speaking Tree. *The Times of India*, May 29, 2011.

Rogers, C. *Freedom to Learn for the '80s*. Columbus: Bell and Howell Company, 1983.

Ruiz, Don Miguel. *The Four Agreements*. San Rafael, CA: Amber-Allen Publishing, Inc., 1997.

"Scientific Foundation of the HeartMath System," accessed June 30, 2019, http://www.heartmath.org/science.

Sylwester, Robert. "How Emotions Affect Learning," in Educational Leadership, vol. 52, no. 2 (October 1994), http://www.ascd.org/publications/educational-leadership/oct94/vol52/num02/How-Emotions-Affect-Learning.aspx

Taylor, Jill Bolte. *My Stroke of Insight: A Brain Scientist's Personal Journey*. New York: Plume, 2009.

Taylor, Shelley. *The Tending Instinct: Women, Men, and the Biology of Our Relationships*. New York: Henry Holt and Company, 2002.

About the Authors

Sue Haynes has taught students in a variety of educational settings, including preschool, elementary school, high school, and college. With master's degrees in special education and literacy, she has focused on empowering at-risk, often highly creative learners who don't fit the mold of standardized education. These experiences led her to write her first book, *Creative Mavericks: Beacons of Authentic Learning.* Sue lives in Tucson, Arizona, where she continues to tutor wonderful "out-of-the-box" kids.

Lisa Plourde sadly passed away at the age of fifty-six. She was an amazing teacher who encouraged her students to follow their dreams. Lisa taught fifth and seventh grade language arts for twenty-seven years, sharing her love of poetry and the joy of language with her students. Her memory continues in the hearts of family, friends, colleagues, and *her students*!

Phyl Brazee is a mother and a grandmother. She started teaching as a remedial-reading teacher, kindergarten through ninth grade. She retired from forty years of holistic teaching as a professor of literacy and multicultural education, as well as fourteen years as the director of a peace and reconciliation studies program. She is passionate about relational, intuitive, heartfelt teaching and learning. She currently resides in upstate New York.

Made in the USA
Monee, IL
01 September 2021